MW00463046

A HISTORY OF KILMAINHAM GAOL
The Dismal House of Little Ease

A HISTORY OF
KILMAINHAM GAOL
The Dismal House of Little Ease

Freida Kelly

Foreword by
John Lonergan

MERCIER PRESS

MERCIER PRESS
PO Box 5, 5 French Church Street, Cork
24 Lower Abbey Street, Dublin 1

© Freida Kelly, 1988

ISBN 0 85342 839 5

First published 1988
Reprinted 1993

Cover illustration: Office of Public Works

Dedication

*This book is dedicated to the memory of my parents,
Michael Kelly and Winnie Atkinson, who taught me to
love history, and to my unique and much loved daughter,
Serena.*

Printed in Ireland by Colour Books, Ltd.

CONTENTS

I know not whether laws be right
or whether laws be wrong
All that we know who lie in Gaol
Is that the wall is strong;
And that each day is like a year
A year whose days are long.

The Ballad of Reading Gaol

– OSCAR WILDE

Foreword

I am delighted to write the introduction to a book which I believe fills a vacuum in relation to the recording of Irish prison history. Accordingly, I welcome this most informative publication and I am certain that it will prove to be of significant educational value for present and future generations. In the book the author has not alone documented the history back from its earliest years in the thirteenth century right through until its closure in 1924, but also has provided indepth profiles and background information on many of the political leaders and personalities who were so closely identified with it.

One of the most striking impressions emanating from the book is that Kilmainham was very much a place of punishment. Equally startling was the obnoxious discrimination which was practised there for many years. Prisoners who could not pay the authorities in some way for their keep were subjected to the most inhuman treatment. The lack of a central administrative control system was also a major deficiency and the regime in Kilmainham very much reflected the attitude of the Governor or Gaoler of the day.

Freida Kelly gives deserved attention to the early nineteenth century activities of the Medical Superintendent, Dr. Edward Trevor, who was probably the most evil influence in the two centuries of Kilmainham Gaol's history. There are fascinating, but horrifying, accounts of his appalling treatment of prisoners and his devious underhand and manipulative methods and activities. Most prisoners committed to Kilmainham during Trevor's reign were placed in an appalling situation and maintaining their mental and physical well-being was the ultimate goal. Not surprisingly many failed to do so even though not condemned to death by the courts but suffered this fate directly as a result of medical neglect and physical abuse.

The prisons of today differ greatly from what they were in the days of Kilmainham. They are now directly under the control of the Minister for Justice, who is personally accountable to Dáil Éireann for the treatment of all persons held in custody. Prisons are now far more open with visiting chaplains, doctors, psychiatrists, psychologists, teachers, social and voluntary workers, etc. Prisons are monitored regularly by Visiting Committees as set up under the 1925 Prisons Visiting Committees Act.

The introduction of the Criminal Justice Act 1960, which provides for the granting of periods of temporary release, enables the Minister for Justice to respond flexibly and positively to most deserving cases. Prisoners can now be released to work, to attend to social and family matters, to continue their education, etc.

All prisoners, with the exception of those sentenced to life imprisonment, are aware of the exact duration of their sentences. This is quite different to the plight of debtors committed to Kilmainham. They were never sure of when they would be released and were held at the whim and mercy of their prosecutor, the creditor. Indeed, one of the most noticeable differences in the actual prison population between today and the early days of Kilmainham is the large decline in the number of debtors and the improvement in the quality of their specific treatment. It appears that in the early nineteenth century, debtors constituted more than half of the prison population and they had the lowest status of all – not even entitled to medical treatment.

Nowadays prison regimes are humane and positive – for example, all prison work is of a productive, educational or training nature and the Kilmainham philosophy of boring, repetitive and non-productive activities is no more. Prisoners are much better cared for medically, physically and mentally, there is no longer dietary punishment, all prisoners receive three full meals a day plus late evening supper; all have free access to doctors and are allowed regular periods of exercise and recreation. They are allowed to have radios, books, hobby work, etc. in their cells to help them manage their time more positively.

However, despite these many real improvements, it must be said some things never change. There is still a severe social stigma attached to those who are imprisoned. Another similarity is that most prisoners come from the poorer classes and most live in the deprived areas within society. Many find it difficult to fully re-integrate upon their release. Prison is still used as a receptacle for society's outcasts and rejects and many times it is a convenient means for society to put those of its problem members 'out of sight and out of mind'.

This book graphically illustrates how alcohol was a major contributing factor to the cause of crime in the days of Kilmainham and this is equally true today. However, alcohol addiction is almost equalled nowadays by the new phenomenon of drug addiction. This is the latest affliction to hit society, bringing with it the dreaded and deadly disease of AIDS. Today, the prison population is made up of large numbers from both groups.

Reading this book makes one aware and grateful for the fact that our present prison system has a far wider range of regimes than in the days of Kilmainham, all of which are more humane and meaningful than the horrific regimes described by the author. While there are still the conventional type prisons, there are also open prisons where prisoners are conditioned to be more responsible for their own behaviour.

I think it is fair to say that prisons have developed positively during the past sixty years or so and are now much better equipped to respond to the needs of the prisoners committed into its care. This book should be a powerful antidote against the arguments of those who today suggest that prisons are too soft and little more than holiday camps. Apart from the psychological pain and social disadvantages experienced by all prisoners, this book with its vivid account of the early atrocities and abuses in Kilmainham brings home to the reader very clearly the absolute need for statutory controls which ensure a basic standard of civilised containment (custody) for society's prisoners.

People committed to prison are very much isolated from and within society, they are segregated from their families, they spend many hours locked alone in their cells, they face huge personal and social problems upon their release. Prisons, no matter how good the physical conditions and services available within, will always be places of punishment.

Fortunately, the regime of Kilmainham, particularly as it was under Dr. Trevor's wicked control, is now history – I hope this book will help ensure that such conditions and their underlying inhuman attitudes will never be part of society's prisons.

John Lonergan
Governor Mountjoy Prison

Introduction

In my very early years of childhood my aunt used to take me by the hand, in a weekly procession to her favourite place of prayer, the grotto at Inchicore.

It was a journey that frightened me as we passed a sombre mass of grey wall at Kilmainham which terrified me and I can clearly remember my aunt utter a half aloud prayer each and every time we passed it.

Many years later, in the comforting presence of my father, I learned about Kilmainham Gaol. For me it was one of the first history lessons of Dublin. My teenage years were spent in learning more about strange grey buildings, with my father's very special talent for storytelling.

As time passed Kilmainham Gaol was taken into care by restoration workers and again with my father, all fright gone, we paid the site a visit. Following his death I left Dublin for some years to work in America.

During this absence from home I seriously began to read about Dublin and its history, and on return to live and work here, retraced the many earlier interesting outings with my father. Inevitably I made my way back to Kilmainham Gaol where work of restoration was now far into its stride. I was too shy at the time to ask if I could join the restoration team, and by 1979 the gaol was fully restored and receiving visitors from all over the world.

I visited there many Sundays in succession. In a sense it was history repeating itself, and I now found myself, in the company of my then nine year old daughter, enthralled by the gaol's historic museum.

During one of those Sunday visits at the end of 1979 I met Mark Hyland, who was then Chairman of the Board of Trustees of Kilmainham Gaol. I learned that he had known my father well, and this prompted me to ask if my interest in history would serve any purpose in Kilmainham Gaol.

For eight years I have been a guide in the gaol and from the outset was determined to discover more of its history.

The Dismal House Of Little Ease is the result of my endeavours, and is offered as an attempt to unlock the fascinating and sometimes gruesome history of the building Dubliners know so well as a landmark.

It was a long task, involving two and a half years of intense research using all official and unofficial sources made available to me. At its completion I have given over to Kilmainham Gaol copies of all documents uncovered during research, and it is hoped that these will make a worthwhile contribution to the Archives of Kilmainham Gaol, currently being set up.

The Dismal House of Little Ease introduced me to an unbelievably rigid administration, and to many hundreds of ordinary Irishmen and Irishwomen who spent time there not because they were criminals, but rather victims of their time.

Kilmainham Gaol today is a unique national monument as well as a surviving statement in Portland and Limestone of the rigid administrative rigours of Dublin in the nineteenth century.

I hope this book will provide an insight into the reason Kilmainham Gaol remains such a singular monument today.

Today, especially, Kilmainham Gaol is a happy building, filled with visitors and a dedicated staff who have a deep commitment to its history, and to each other.

I am very proud to be part of that team.

Freida Kelly

1. The Beginning

The earliest traces of a prison in the area known as Kilmainham, on the tilted edge of Dublin's South Circular Road, revert to the opening years of the thirteenth century, when the Hospitaller Knights of St. John of Jerusalem established the Castle and Manor House of Kilmainham, in the year 1210 AD. The lands on which they erected the Irish priory for their wealthy religious community were a bequest to the knights by their founder, Earl Richard FitzGilbert, Strongbow.

The transmission of all the lands on which the Castle and Manor Priory House of Kilmainham were established can be dated and verified as taking place in the year 1174 as they were produced by the Knights in evidence in a case before a Dublin jury in 1261, concerning a major disagreement over fishing rights between the Hospitaller Knights and the city of Dublin.[1] The Charter of Grant, bestowing 'All the lands of Kylmaynham' to the Knights bore the date 1174 and proved, beyond doubt, ownership of the lands and all rights thereto, in favour of the Hospitaller Community, two years before Strongbow's death in 1176.[2]

Before reaching Dublin, the rivers Liffey and Camac join at Kilmainham, having danced downwater in the direction of Dublin city at a distance of some seven hundred yards apart. On the plateau above where the rivers joined in confluence, the Hospitaller Knights of St. John of Jerusalem erected the House or Castle of Kilmainham, the official residence of the grand prior of the order in Ireland, with his staff of knights, squires, chaplains, clerks and 'inferior attendants in great number and variety'.[3] From Kilmainham, the Irish prior (usually an Englishman) administered the duties and responsibilities essential to the growth of the order in Ireland. In his frequent absences his deputy, the preceptor of Kilmainham, assumed the full responsibility of prior.

The hospitaller knights were an order of much wealth and possessions, while the rich lands on which the Priory House and Castle of Kilmainham stood embraced an area of just over two miles. Accommodation for the community was situated within an inner enclosure, containing the Castle, (official residence of the Irish Grand Prior) and the preceptor of Kilmainham. A number of detached buildings, including an internal chapel and small private quarters for the preceptor, along with several dormitories for the brethren were also bound within the inner circle. Some of the highly placed templar knights merited their own self-contained apartments nearby.

The entire area was cloistered by a surrounding quadrangle of strong walls, towers and an outer ditch. The order in Ireland was a tier-structured one, completely self supporting and was as impregnable as any solid fortress. An outer enclosure featured thick secure walls, while a deep wide ditch closed around the living quarters of the lay brothers and 'inferior attendants'. This comprised a courthouse, stables, laundry, as well as a prison – *Tetra Domus De Malrepos* – The Dismal House of Little Ease.[4]

This is the earliest record of a prison situated at Kilmainham. There appears to be no evidence or trace of an exchange flow of traffic nor do any records survive necessary for the movement or transfer of prisoners. It seems likely that this in its time was a prison of 'Care' – an asylum provided within the scope of the healing work of the Knights of St. John – a human scrapyard for the confinement of the unfortunates of the day, declared by court or family authorities as of little ease within the mind. The custodial care provided by the knights, commonplace within most monasteries of the time, would remove from the family circle the threatening presence of insanity, always associated with evil, restoring ease of mind to the home or community circle.

The practice of treating mentally disturbed members of Dublin society humanely would not come about until nearly one hundred years after the death in 1745 of Jonathan Swift, writer, wit and satirist, author of *Gulliver's Travels* and Dean of St. Patrick's Cathedral, Dublin. His will would contain instructions and money for the establishment of St. Patrick's Hospital to be erected 'for the care of aged lunaticks and other diseased persons' situated one mile from Kilmainham, towards the city of Dublin. In the meantime the prisons of Ireland would remain crowded with the unfortunate sufferers of disorders affecting the mind.

The hospitaller knights retained their growing Irish priory home at Kilmainham, as their order flourished throughout Ireland, until the suppression of the monasteries by Henry VIII from 1536. The Kilmainham property was seized by the throne of Henry in 1540 and lay idle and unoccupied for almost one hundred years, until finally renovated in the seventeenth century as a potential home for the Irish lord lieutenant and his staff at the cost of £100 to the Treasury.[5] The vice-regal parties refused to occupy the demesne, claiming it was damp from disuse, unfit for human habitation and would make vice-regal life burdensome, because of its distance from Dublin Castle.

Henry, fourth son of Cromwell, kept a hunting-lodge in the Kilmainham grounds from time to time. His presence in the neighbourhood of Kilmainham is ironic, since it was this Cromwell who introduced the idea of the transportation ships, which for over half a century provided a dense traffic of Irish people destined for distant strange shores on a royal order of banishment – issued lavishly as a regal and merciful alternative to hanging.

His Majesty, Charles II established the Royal Hospital, Kilmainham on the site of the ruined manor priory house. The hospital was for the accommodation of retired or wounded soldiers, designed by William Robinson and completed between 1680-1694.[6]

As the seventeenth century drew breath upon its closing years, the district of Kilmainham, in the county of Dublin, in full view of the west wall of His Majesty's Royal Hospital, became known as Gallows Hill, from the movement there of a gallows which had been for several years situated at nearby Parkgate Street.[7] Prison accommodation in Ireland at the same period was notoriously lacking in any sort of morality, performing only a holding operation for its dense population in respite between sentence and execution and gruesomely cloistered in the realms of underground dungeons, or within the towers of city gates, most notably in the capital within the infamous tower of Dublin Castle.[8]

Public floggings, whippings, pillories and stocks, exhibited the attitude of justice not only being done, but being seen to be done. Public executions were held almost daily.[9] All methods used were to demonstrate publicly the awful consequences of offences against the royal administration within the kingdom of Ireland.

James Butler, First Duke of Ormonde, and the first Irishman to receive a Dukedom from the Crown, returning to Dublin in 1662 was the prime motivator of the period of restoration which developed Dublin as a city of major growth. The formation of the Royal Park, for the King's Deer and later re-named the Phoenix Park, was high on Ormonde's list of restoration projects. The relocation of the county gallows from Parkgate Street to Kilmainham was a necessary cosmetic move, because of the former site's proximity to the entrance to the Royal Deer Park. The spectacle of a living man gasping his last breath in a contrived and public fashion was not a pretty sight to set before any visiting king.[10]

The long term formation of the King's Deer Park was finalised in 1747 by Lord Chesterfield, while the gaols of the kingdom of Ireland, in particular the old decaying county gaol of Dublin situated at Kilmainham are found in the latter half of the eighteenth century, diseased, overcrowded, hived with vermin. They were fed daily a diet of male and female debtors and criminals who through drink and oblivion could black out their bodily pain, but the commercial violence of the extortion of fees by gaolers raged rampant.

The prisons of Ireland were run as exploitive hostels. Prisoners were delivered into the hands of their gaolers as assets to be stripped, while rules were far less evident on the interior of prison walls than was the display of the Tables of Fees.[11]

2. The Old Gaol

On 15 September 1782, George Grenville Nugent Temple was appointed Lord Lieutenant of Ireland.[1] One of the first directives Temple issued from his office was an instruction to all county sheriffs asking them to report back to his chief secretary 'as a matter of urgency' on the state and conditions within their prisons.

Many gaols of the time were located within run down property, long in the ownership of the crown, and hurriedly converted after long disuse into a prison. Repairs were minimal, if carried out at all. Other gaols were privately owned, (the Bishop of Ely owned Ely Gaol) and conditions within all prisons depended entirely upon the proprietor to carry out any and every repair.[2] What was certain was that all needed drastic reform in structure, administration and finance, and none more so than the old county gaol of Dublin, at Kilmainham, now situated within the ruined confines of the once Grand Manor Priory House of the hospitaller knights.

Temple's direction was met with some fear and much apprehension. Those who were officially required to examine the state and conditions of the prison hovels in Ireland seldom did so, while gaol fever, caused by free flowing sewage, damp and dank crowded conditions, festered by a bad prison diet, compounded the problem. Few officials were courageous enough to examine the interior of these maps of mystery, carrying out their duty from the exterior of the prison only and processing complaints from prisoners in the form of written prisoners' petitions. Some of these never saw the outside of the prison walls and most never reached their designated destination the lord lieutenant's office in Dublin Castle.

In 1783, the old Kilmainham Gaol was a low-lying decrepit building, falling apart from lack of maintenance and repair, with foundations weakened and insecure from its close proximity to the river Camac. It was frequently and easily flooded. It was located in Old Kilmainham Lane on the low-lying portion of the neighbourhood of Kilmainham.[3] The Ordnance Survey Name Book refers to its situation as 'Kilmainham Lane, Old, on the Cork and Waterford Road, running east and west, beginning at Mount Brown'. The site is shown on the 1911 edition of the twenty-five inch ordnance survey map and was situated opposite the present Brookfield Road, where it joins the district of Old Kilmainham.

The state of disrepair of the old Kilmainham Gaol is borne out in a report furnished by the then gaoler, to the county sheriff in 1784, relating an account of an unsuccessful attempt at escape by several of the inmates: 'I rounded them up and secured them as best as this wretched gaol that I keep will allow me to'.[4] The 'wretched gaol' he was referring to was notorious for its atrocious state and had the reputation of being one of the toughest gaols in the kingdom of Ireland.

The old gaol featured four cage-like dungeons, referred to as 'Towers' from the days when prisons were neatly tucked into tower gates, at the entrance to a city, as in London's Newgate. Their small narrow windows were level with the ground and within these caged compounds, which always faced street level, were confined all grades of prisoners, male, female and children. There was no acknowledgement of creed or class in the debtors' section, and no segregation of the sexes, not even at night.[5] Most of the prisoners, women as well as men were bound, sometimes for long periods, 'loaded with irons'.

Debtors' dungeons frequently occupied an overspan of class, embracing both the vulgar and the exalted spectrums of society. In London's Old Fleet Prison, Sir Francis Engelsfield took three chambers where he received upwards of sixty visitors a day, but no such good account survives in relation to the Old County Dublin Gaol, which housed mostly Catholics and always the poor debtor prisoner.[6] In Kilmainham, as in other prisons, the gaoler ruled with a masterful tyranny, dishing out the bare necessities of straw, bread and water in return for his fees, while the destitute occupant of the tower compounds unable to procure payment of fees from family or friends had all rights eroded as he embarked on a weak path to starvation, brutality, fever, destitution and often death.

In 1773 John Howard was appointed sheriff of Bedford. He was appalled at the conditions prisoners had to endure, some for very paltry debts and found the county gaol diseased with vermin and over-crowded with the despairing inmates. He was very soon familiar with the illegal fee system in operation there and having talked with some of the gaolers, found that their salaries were not enough to meet the requirements of providing food and straw. Howard immediately embarked on a campaign for a regular and liveable wage for gaolkeepers, convinced that this step would eliminate the system of fees extorted from prisoners by gaolers.[7]

He placed a proposal before the town council that the fees for prisoners should be paid for by the county, rather than by the prisoner. Asked to provide the county magistrates with a precedent for this, he visited the neighbouring gaols of Cambridge and Huntingdon to discover that the system was in operation there too. Within a short time Howard had visited almost every English prison, and was to devote the next nineteen years delving into dungeons providing the data on a prison by prison basis which resulted in the gaol reforms of 1779. By 1777 the information Howard had collected was mustered together and published in Warrington as *The State of the Prisons*. While work was in progress on the new Kilmainham Gaol, Howard's book had gone into its fourth edition, containing particulars of each prison in Ireland and England. The new County of Dublin Gaol at Kilmainham would bear strongly the evidence and influence of Howard.

In 1778 Howard visited the old Kilmainham Gaol, where he was appalled at the fee system in operation there and paid the fees of acquittal for several young male inhabitants who were rotting in the dungeons for misdemeanour. During this visit on 28 March, he found eight debtors and 47 others in the decrepit gaol building.

The seasoned inmates of the old Kilmainham Gaol were a motley rowdy crowd who practised the threat of 'Garnish' money. This was an enforced and hollow tax imposed on the new prisoner, guaranteeing his safety in return for whatever money he had attached to his person. It was a strip-or-pay situation. If the new prisoner could not meet this demand, then his clothes were stripped forcefully from his person leaving those in already dire need and want in a state of naked indignity. In fear of the seasoned prison bully most newcomers succumbed to the pressure. Following the garnish of a newcomer, a bout of hopeless drinking would ensue.

The plight of the naked newcomer was hardly likely to reach official ears, while the wretched prisoner stripped of his clothing would remain in need and nakedness behind the locked tower doors, opened only to admit a newcomer, for a rowdy inhabitant to be clamped into irons or for a fevered or dead body to be removed. The money obtained by the act of 'Garnish' would, whenever possible, be passed through the narrow street-facing grating and be used to purchase illegal whiskey, readily available to the depraved prisoners at fourpence a half pint from loitering hawkers.[8]

Howard on a second visit to Kilmainham early one morning in June 1787 found the inmates 'all drunk at 11 am' while on yet another visit he arrived just in time one evening to prevent a fire starting on the straw where they lay together in a combined state of sleep and intoxication.

The hopeless ensemble fought with each other continuously, in order to secure a place at the street-facing grating, where they could beseech solace from the charitable passers-by during the day. Confused and in differing stages of fear and frenzy, they spent their waking hours begging for food, pleading for liquor to take away consciousness, fight fever and ease pain. They incessantly cried out to the passing gentry to supply them with the tools to escape, or for assistance in the payment of their fees. They cursed loudly those who paid no heed to their miserable cries.

In London's notorious Newgate in the early eighteenth century there were two gratings facing street level called 'Giggers' which were used for begging or as an assembly point for acquaintances, and of course for the purchase of supplies from an adjoining shop. Another method in the debtors' section of Dublin's Newgate completed in 1783 was a boot on a string left dangling from the upper storeys of the gaol, while in Exeter Gaol fettered prisoners were released into the street with a begging bowl, or shackled to the prison wall.[9]

Debtor prisoners fared worst. Their sentences were of uncertain duration, depending entirely upon the attendance of their prosecutor in court to give evidence of the sometimes paltry debt owed to him. If he did not make an appearance in court, due to a previous engagement the debtor prisoner would be returned to the dungeon compound while his gaol board charges continued to increase.

Debtor prisoners received no food allowance in any of His Majesty's prisons. They were served water soup – bread boiled in water – three times a day, while in the event of a prosecutor feeling sympathy or remorse, the gaoler would not grant the prisoner his freedom until his gaol fees, which were mounting daily, were paid in full. All classifications of prisoners, except debtors, also received medical attention.

Debtors who could work were allowed to do so in Kilmainham, in certain circumstances. They were not, however, permitted to undertake any labouring work with the assistance of tools, which their gaolers feared they would use as a prop to escape, or to get up to any other mischief. Any digging that had to be done by a working debtor was negotiated with his bare hands.[10] As the old Kilmainham Gaol was a county gaol it functioned as a stop-over point for convicts about to be delivered to the transportation ships, berthed at Ringsend and at Kingstown, on the coastline of Dublin.

The best rooms of the gaol complex, set apart from the debtor's dungeons, accommodated the accompanying military escort. His Majesty's soldiers, bruised from battles bloody or the approach of old age, were now settled into the Royal Hospital, Kilmainham, as well as any extra troops needed for the safeguarding of the prisons of Ireland.[11]

In the light of the new modern thinking, Dublin gaol reform, although on its way through parliament and the subject of several heated parliamentary debates greatly influenced by John Howard, was overdue in the gaols of Ireland.

3. The Dismal House

By the early 1770s Dublin's population was upwards of 153,000. The development of the city as a major European entity, begun a century ago by James Butler, First Duke of Ormonde, continued.[1]

The Wide Streets Commission of 1757 responsible for the present structure of Dublin's streets, with emphasis on the major thoroughfare, Sackville Street, had altered the city's pace dramatically. Dublin's North and South Quays were now set out, with access north to south of the city by the erection of several bridges across the River Liffey making commercial life easier and causing the movement of trade and traffic to alter radically.[2]

Grafton Street was becoming the centre of fashion, education and commerce. Dublin now proudly displayed its handsome new public buildings, notably its new law courts, the Four Courts, designed by Gandon. The Customs House moved to its present location nearer to the mouth of the River Liffey. City Hall strategically established itself in close proximity to the administrative centre of Irish life, beside Dublin Castle.

Many Irish prisons were insecure, but since security within the prison building came from the purchase of ironmongery and fetters restraining movement, no great emphasis was placed on the building of the prison complex .[3]

Following publication of Howard's *State of the Prisons*, detailing the accommodation of each prison in England and Ireland as well as the number of prisoners, where and how they worked and for how long, under what conditions they ate and slept, the prisons of the kingdom passed from the unknown to the known. His work was the first effective instrument in the case for reform and rebuilding, showing conditions within prison walls to be an astonishingly uniform but uniformly astonishing.

For a number of years, John Howard had immersed himself full-time into his crusade for prison reform, laying emphasis on the separate cell accommodation system, and the strengthening of the prison building. Yearly his campaign gained momentum, while his reform plans were acceded to sometimes with surprisingly brief negotiations, since Howard's person from close proximity to prisoners was beginning to smell as bad as the prisons he sought to reform.

Howard would emerge as a distinct influence on the shaping of the new Kilmainham, which would play host to Irish men and Irish women until it finally closed its doors in 1924, never to re-open as a prison again. He intended the introduction of morality into the prison administration, merging the form of the prison building with the events that took place inside it, by an arranged marriage of mortar and morality.

In Dublin, Sir Edward Newenham, MP, who had been bestowed with a knighthood in 1764, was campaigning for better gaol conditions for the county. Possibly under the influence of Howard and certainly influenced by the new-look Dublin city, he believed it was 'time to think anew with regard to gaol conditions within the county'.[4] He had petitioned Parliament in 1774 with this aim in mind, but the Exchequer was unimpressed. It was not until 1786 that any progress was made in seeking further gaol accommodation when Luke Gardiner, Senior Member of Parliament for the county of Dublin and a resident of Dublin's Phoenix Park, petitioned the House for the widening of roads in the county. This bill contained provisions for the erection of a new gaol in the county of Dublin, at Kilmainham.[5] Luke Gardiner's plea was presented to the House by Sir Edward Newenham and in March of 1786 became law. It included a budget for the provision of gallows' equipment, chains, iron fetters, muffs and handcuffs.

The architect selected to design the new gaol was John Traile, a resident of nearby Islandbridge, at whose home the lord lieutenant and Dublin Castle officials dined frequently.[6] As the old Kilmainham Gaol was by this time in a further state of deterioration and unsafe for the custody of any great number of prisoners, it was anticipated that work would begin immediately following approval of Traile's plan by the lord lieutenant and the grand jury of Dublin county. Dublin's Newgate Prison opened its doors for the reception of prisoners in February of 1783 during the short reign of Nugent Temple as lord lieutenant.[7] It would display, as would Kilmainham at its completion Temple's exclusive 'Hanging Plank' as a gruesome eye-catcher above the main entrance.[8] Within months of the opening of Newgate, John Howard would argue publicly against its design and administration, advocating that it had in use underground dungeons which he wanted to eradicate from the system completely.[9]

The 26th Act of His Majesty George III was satisfied that 'The Common of Kilmainham, in the area known as Gallows Hill was a most suitable site for the erection of the New County Gaol' since it was on a height, necessarily close to water, and had an unrestricted circulation of air. The Common was free from other buildings in the immediate vicinity, except for the secluded Royal Hospital. The Exchequer was prepared to fund the venture to the sum of £953.16.2d, further agreeing that the old prison should be put on the market for public sale, the proceeds from which were to be lodged in the newly established Bank of Ireland 'For County Use'.[10]

Sir Nicholas Lawless, later the first Lord Cloncurry and Lord of the Manor of Kilmainham, donated the site for the new county of Dublin prison, at a fee of £1 sterling per year, payable to his heirs and assigns forever. The deed of conveyance for the acquisition of the site from Sir Nicholas Lawless, to the Rt. Honourable Luke Gardiner, now high sheriff of Dublin, is dated 19 September, 1786. It empowered all the necessary instructions for the erection of the gaol and for making the necessary approaches, such as yards and offices.[11]The deed defines the site as:

All that and those the centre of that part of the Barony of the Common of Kilmainham called 'Gallows Hill' situate lying and being in the Barony of Newcastle in the County of Dublin, bounded on the East by the Circular Road, on the West by the road to the Black Lion Turnpike, on the North leading from the road to the

Royal Hospital, to Inchicore, and on the South by the
Mill Race containing in front to the North 320 feet, to the
East 125 feet and to the West 222 feet, making in the
whole one acre and nine perches.

The Dublin grand jury were empowered to levy the county at
the terms of Michaelmas and Easter for any additional
necessary finances the building of the new gaol would require or
merit. Residents of the neighbourhood were also given the
option of presenting a petition before the Court of King's Bench
should any of them believe that pipes carrying water to the
gaol from the nearby Grand Canal and crossing their land
constituted a dangerous or objectionable practise.[12] However,
with an address in the county of Dublin which sported a public
gallows as a neighbourhood centrepiece, which doubtless
dictated by its very existence all community thought and
actions, perhaps the least said in objection, the better.

It was as well that the residents remained silent, for plans
for the supply of water to the new prison changed during the
early months of design. It was decided instead to draw water
for laundry and domestic use from the River Liffey by the
installation of a pump at Islandbridge, bringing water to the
Royal Hospital as well, with the cost of installation shared by
both institutions. Drinking water was provided for in the plans
by the digging of a well within the prison walls seventy feet
below ground level.

John Howard again visited the old Kilmainham Gaol and
found it rotting beyond any further secure usefulness. He was
shown Traile's plans and believed them to be inadequate, not
well enough thought out in concept, and providing grossly
insufficient cell accommodation on the separate occupancy
principle. He had great fears that the project would digress
along the lines of default as Dublin's Newgate had done. He
advocated that not enough consideration was given to the area
of the new prison which was to be used as a government depot
for convicts awaiting transportation, and whose stay at the
prison could be lengthy while the details of those hazardous
journeys, weather and vessels permitting, were worked out.

As Traile went back to his drawing board, parliament was

presented with a petition in the Irish House of Commons advising of the additional expense of labour and materials: the revised plan would require in excess of £18,000, comprising 52 separate cells and modern roomy accommodation for the debtor prisoner. That was the plan. The reality would be something quite different.

The persistence of Sir Edward Newenham brought this petition once again to parliament, which remained further unimpressed and unmoved. The chancellor believed that the expenses incurred in building a new prison for any county should come from the funds of that county, and not from the exchequer. Newenham, undaunted, and with the assistance of Mr Justice Day, the Earl of Carhampton and several other county gentlemen spearheaded a finance drive which would see the new gaol completed without further recourse to the county public purse.

Coinciding with John Howard's untimely death in 1791 prior to seeing completion of work on the project, Theobald Wolfe Tone founded the Society of United Irishmen, in Belfast 'to break the connection with England, the never failing source of all our political evils'.[13] By 1795 it was an effective and massively populated secret society with a Protestant middle core and a manifesto designed to unite Catholic and Protestant Irishmen, but above all to strive together in unity for independence from British rule. Ireland was now greatly affected by the aftermath of the French Revolution and with the United Irishmen closing ranks, 1,000 extra troops were drafted into Ireland to defend the kingdom in Ireland against insurrectionists.

The Earl of Carhampton, who had succeeded Abercrombie as commander-in-chief despatched a courier to London, with the information that the new county of Dublin gaol was in an ideal location at Kilmainham to house extra troops and was in full view of His Majesty's ammunition fort in the Phoenix Park. There are no official reports in existence to establish whether the military ever occupied the gaol, while newspaper accounts in November 1795 declare the prison to be 'very nearly completed'.

The 'New Prison' as it was called and often confused with

Newgate, received its first prisoners on 12 August 1796. The official opening ceremony was attended by the high sheriff of Dublin, along with Sir Edward Newenham and several justices of the peace 'and a great number of other gentlemen, who dined by invitation afterwards in Harrington's of Grafton Street'.[14]

It was an august occasion loaded with irony for Sir Edward Newenham, who before too much time would pass, would find himself writing from a prison cell at the gaol he had so earnestly striven to see established.

The Dismal House of Little Ease had opened its doors once more.

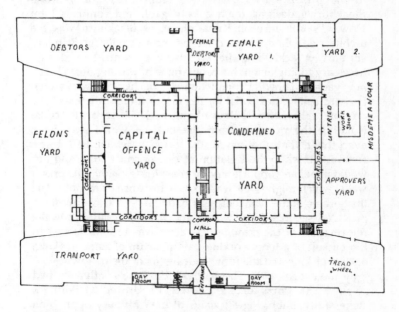

Plan of the Ground Floor of Kilmainham Gaol 1796 showing 27 separate cells and Central Administration block. The large yard to the left of the entrance on the side of the prison nearest to the courthouse was the area of departure for convicts awaiting transportation to Botany Bay, and the shores of America. (Drawing by Martin Crawford.)

4. Doors Open and Close

The new Kilmainham Gaol was ready for occupation in August of 1796, five years after Howard's death, but the Reformer would have been well pleased with the completed project.

The central building which forms part of the main entrance to the prison shows Architect Traile's use of William Blackburn's designs for a county gaol, and confirms John Howard's influence on Kilmainham, as Blackburn was the architect on whom Howard leaned most heavily for help and support in achieving the architectural control of design necessary to implement his programme of prison reform.[1] The new gaol contained at completion all the characteristics which Howard believed essential for the successful reformation of the criminal character. Kilmainham had 52 separate cells, isolating the prisoner from the outside world and from everything that motivated the offence which had been committed, while the isolation of one prisoner from another would annul any opportunity for conspiracies within the prison walls, which might later lead to a disturbance or to riot.[2] The thirty-three and a half foot high boundary walls of limestone provided security from within and from without, while the reformation of the criminal character was to be achieved in the pursuit of a long working day made up of stonebreaking, oakum-picking and the futile endeavours of the treadwheel.

By the end of 1795 Theobald Wolfe Tone's influence had swelled the ranks of the Society of United Irishmen, successfully embracing all walks of life. Military oppression brought the small tenant farmer into membership, while small homesteaders were frequently looted for fuel, firearms and food.[3] The exclusion of Roman Catholics from taking a Parliamentary seat remained a burning issue.

England's view was hostile to any immediate changes and when William Wentworth Fitzwilliam was despatched to

Ireland to take up the position of lord chancellor, he was instructed to make no administrative changes in relation to Catholics. Neither did Fitzwilliam attempt to discourage the Catholic demands, thereby drawing the continuous attention of the cabinet to the necessity for urgent and immediate reform. To demonstrate that the Catholic population of Ireland formed an important nucleus of the kingdom of Ireland, in token fashion, the Royal College of St Patrick's at Maynooth, Co. Kildare was established towards the end of 1795 for the education of Roman Catholic clergy throughout the English speaking world.[4]

Prisoners entering Kilmainham Gaol for the first time came through the front door. As they stepped from the gaol delivery cart, bound in irons, some hungry, dirty and diseased from anything up to an eight day hold-over in one of the city's notorious bridewells, they huddled together in fear at the first sight of their awesome surroundings, watched always by a curious passing traffic who came to peer inquisitively. Well-endowed coaches and fours trotted past from the direction of the newly established North and South Circular Roads, or from the fashionable Phoenix Park nearby.

Claiming the attention of all those who passed or entered the thick steel enforced door were the Five Devils of Kilmainham emblazoned in bronze above the front entrance to the prison. The creator of this work is unknown, as is its origin, although such gruesome and tasteless decorative works were not unknown or uncommon above the front entrance of prisons of that time. Above the door of London's notorious Newgate were five large bronze keys, encircled in five chains.[5] In the case of Kilmainham the work is believed to symbolise the devils of crime, restrained by the chains of justice.

The east and west wings of the prison were broken into corridors of high security, housing the condemned prisoners and capital offenders awaiting trial. These categories took air and exercise in the yards encircled by their cell blocks, never together, and always in silence. Separate accommodation was also blocked off for prisoners under sentence of hard labour, while the felons and misdemeanours were huddled together in

The Five Devils of Kilmainham, a detail in bronze above the front entrance. Artist unknown but the work is supposed to represent the demons of crime restrained by the chains of justice. (Drawing by Martin Crawford.)

outbuildings adjacent to their working areas.[6]

From the beginning the debtor's section within the new prison was overused and became as densely populated as the hollowed hovel in Old Kilmainham Lane that it had been intended to replace. This was sectioned off into 'master' and 'pauper' accommodation and classification depended entirely upon the amount of money paid to the gaoler for board. The side of the prison nearest to the courthouse was set aside for the convicts waiting to board transportation ships or prison hulks berthed on the coast of Dublin at Kingstown and at Ringsend. Juveniles were slotted in separate accommodation below ground level, whenever possible, whereas a portion of the prison was set aside for the incarceration of unfortunate lunatics.

Male and female prisoners were not allowed to come together, either at recreation or during working hours. In each separate section of the gaol, space was allotted whenever necessary or possible for the hospitalisation of the sick.

In Kilmainham each prisoner housed in the east and west wings slept alone in his single cell at night on a plank bed. During the day he was forced to participate in silence in a programme of 'industrious' labour, under the watchful eye of a heavy military guard. The prisoner who was declared too lame or too infirm by the prison doctor, worked from his cell, engaged in the picking of oakum.[7]

In the new county of Dublin gaol, the state prisoner was deprived of everything save his cell bible. However, no prison regime could deprive him of his memories – and his cause.

Kilmainham's first gaoler was Robert Ware (sometimes called Weir) who from the accounts that survive of his short influence on the prison was a kindly man.[8] Within days of the official opening of the gaol, Ware received into his custody several prisoners including a number of debtor prisoners. Also to the new gaol came Leonard Hicks, the gaoler of the Gaol of St. Sepulchre in Dublin's New Street, sent to Kilmainham for the extortion of fees from prisoners, confirming, no doubt, that reform within the prison administration within the kingdom of Ireland was alive and well.[9] An unnamed dentist, in attempting to extract the tooth of a local magistrate, broke it, and was slapped into one of the dungeons in Kilmainham, on a charge of high treason.

The Society of United Irishmen had now enlarged their ranks yet further. Tone's influence was nationwide but unrest, particularly in the northern counties, and predominantly in the county of Antrim, was present. Henry Joy McCracken in his native Belfast was one of the leading organisers of Tone's movement in the north and was preparing the men of his county for revolt.

On 6 October 1796, Gaoler Ware received into custody Henry Joy McCracken, and on the following day the prisoner appeared before Justice Boyd, charged with high treason and was given over to Ware's care for an indefinite period.[10]

By December of that year, eleven men, including Henry's brother, William and Henry Haslett, a Belfast shipbroker, were also in Kilmainham charged with high treason. Kilmainham Gaol was developing its political identity.

Christmas 1796 was not a cheerless occasion in Kilmainham, when filtering in to the prison came the news that Wolfe Tone, at the head of 6,000 French troops had reached Bantry Bay in Co. Cork. Unfavourable weather and disunity among the leaders prevented the contingent from landing, but the fact that they had, in spite of the vigilant British navy, been able to make their way as far as Bantry, alarmed the government, and boosted the morale of the Kilmainham state prisoners, turning Christmas behind bars into a season of cheerfulness and blind optimism.

In later months Henry Joy McCracken's health deteriorated drastically within his bare prison cell, but under Gaoler Ware he received kindly treatment. On the instructions of the government, Ware had been told to 'provide them with any necessity they might want' and it seems from an unpaid statement submitted to the government by the gaoler amounting in all to £1,086 for items of 'drink, diet, washing, coals, etc.', Ware did just that.

Communication for the state prisoners, although in solitary confinement and in silence, was not difficult. Henry Joy McCracken devised the ingenious method of sharing his claret by placing the bottle on a piece of string. This was cushioned by a sock, or a shirt sleeve, and eased out of the unglazed cell window, into the eagerly waiting hands of men whiling their last miserable hours away in the condemned yard, while the guard's eye was turned. Having shared a drop, the bottle would enter unseen through another cell window.

But Kilmainham Gaol had a sixth demon, left freely to roam its dark corridors in the person of the new medical superintendent of prisons – Edward Trevor, appointed to the post in the early months of 1797. Trevor would base himself at Kilmainham, and immediately work his way into assuming complete authority. Upon the administration of Kilmainham, Edward Trevor was to have a lasting and drastic effect.

Robert Ware was dismissed from the prison, following the escape of three prisoners, who walked out through the front door, unchallenged, disappearing into the backwoods of the district. Kilmainham's second gaoler was an army man, John Richardson, who with his wife Susannah, and their three young children moved into the gaoler's roomy apartment in the central building, to commence his career in the manner of his predecessor.[11]

But Edward Trevor had other plans.

Unrest and uneasiness became the order of the day within the walls of Kilmainham because of Trevor's tyrannical manner. He immediately set about organising his network of spies within the prison walls, while outside, about the entire country, the winds of rebellion were blowing hard. On 27 July 1797, Henry Haslett is found writing from his solitary cell to the government to remind them – 'Four law terms in the courts have passed without any Bill of Indictment being brought against me', while his health deteriorated as he waited for trial.[12] Haslett was finally bailed on 11 January 1798, along with Henry Joy McCracken. His brother William was released on a high bail a short time later. All returned to their native Belfast to organise the men of the north for the oncoming revolt. For Henry Joy McCracken, this return to Belfast was to be a fateful journey, ultimately leading to the gallows.

Dublin Castle now had in its employment a new and valuable informer in Thomas Reynolds, whose wife was a sister of Mrs Theobald Wolfe Tone.[13] Reynolds himself belonged to the inner ranks of the society and had tipped the Castle off through the Dublin trader, Cope, to whom he was indebted, about an important meeting of the executive which was to take place at noon on 12 March 1798 at the quayside home of the Dublin merchant, Oliver Bond.

The spectacular arrest of Thomas Addis Emmet one of the executive members of the Leinster Directory of the Society of United Irishmen was effected from the family home on fashionable Stephen's Green, Dublin, early on the morning of 12 March as he was on his way to the executive meeting.

At both Stephen's Green and Oliver Bond's house the raiders searched intensively for the newly moulded seal of the Society – designed by Tom Emmet's younger brother, Robert. At the Emmet household the soldiers took some of the children from their beds in case the seal was concealed on their person, but Tom's wife Jane had it safely hidden about her person.

On 13 March 1798, into Gaoler Richardson's custody in Kilmainham – following the raid on Bond's house – came Laurence Kelly from Portlaoise, Edward Henry and Hugh Jackson, Richard Dillon – a Dublin merchant, Patrick Devine – a wealthy county Dublin farmer, and Peter Ivers – an important executive member of the society. Thomas Addis Emmet would leave Kilmainham for the confines of Fort George Prison Camp in Scotland, under the Banishment Act introduced in June of that year.

By late April 1798 the signs of rebellion were evident everywhere, and an insurrection did take place on 23 May 1798 in Dublin, despite the enormous drawback of the arrest of Lord Edward Fitzgerald, one of the principal leaders. Ironically, Lord Edward had never been a prisoner in Kilmainham, but had entered its dark corridors once during Gaoler Ware's administration as a visitor, and was caught short when Doctor Trevor arrived to make an impromptu survey of the gaol. Lord Edward was bundled into one of the cells, while the danger passed for Gaoler Ware.[14]

In Dublin, the plan had been to gain control of the city by first of all taking Dublin Castle. The day passed without even an attempt on this, and Dublin and the rest of the province of Leinster were suppressed swiftly by military forces, filling the gaols of Newgate and Kilmainham to bursting point.

Morale in Kilmainham during July 1798 was particularly low among the state prisoners, not only because of the failure of the Rising but because of the ceaseless number of executions, including the two young Cork lawyers, John and Henry Sheares who were taken from their Kilmainham cells and publicly executed together outside Newgate prison, in Green Street. Gaoler Richardson, on instructions from government to relieve the prisoner congestion within the prison, set out for the county of Kildare with a number of prisoners, bound for the gaol of Naas. It was a hazardous journey, made in very bad winter weather, and on his return to Kilmainham on 13 November he found his wife and family frightened by the atmosphere in the gaol. Prison discipline had broken down completely and verged on riot. Richardson immediately set about restoring order to the prison complex and finally, after two nights without sleep, was forced to bed with a raging fever.[15]

Susannah Richardson nursed him through that night, and finally had to call on Doctor Trevor to come to the bedside of her delirious husband. The medical superintendent of the prison refused to see the sick gaoler on discovering that Richardson had not yet received his money from the government and could not pay him. Finally Trevor relented when the distraught wife offered the inspector a pair of silver mounted pistols, which he accepted as payment for medical care.

In spite of his wife's intensive devotion, John Richardson died in his fevered bed in Kilmainham, on 20 November 1798. Within hours of his funeral, his grief-stricken widow was herself a victim of fever. For the second time the medical superintendent was called to the gaoler's apartment, and for the second time, even under such extenuating circumstances, Doctor Trevor – medical doctor – refused the call, until the sick woman offered him a horse belonging to her late husband, valued at £25 – the equivalent of one year of John Richardson's salary.

Susannah Richardson recovered and spent a harrowing and nervous Christmas barricaded into the apartment she had happily, some months ago, moved into with her husband,

while Doctor Trevor busied himself with plans to have the
hapless woman thrown on to the roadside.   With the
assistance of the sheriff of the county of Dublin, he was
eventually successful and Susannah Richardson, along with
her three fatherless children found themselves forcibly
evicted. One year later from her sister's home in Dublin's King
Street, she was still petitioning the government for amounts of
salary and expenditure due to her late husband for items
purchased on Secretary Cooke's instructions for the needs of the
state prisoners.

The tyrannical reign of Doctor Edward Trevor was now about
to begin in earnest. Richardson was replaced by the doctor's
own man, George Dunn. Not surprisingly, Dunn had a
background of military training and is known to have been a
turnkey at Mullingar gaol. The connection between Dunn and
Trevor was bizarre. Trevor had been having an affair with
gaoler Dunn's wife for many years, an extra-marital
association condoned, it seems, by the new gaoler of
Kilmainham. Like their predecessors, the Dunn's occupied the
gaoler's apartment, but Mrs. Dunn did not take any act or part
in assisting with the administration or domestic running of the
prison.[16]

George Dunn for his endeavours and long loyalty to Trevor,
would become Kilmainham's first governor, following the
passing of the Prisons Act 1826, giving over the control of
prisons solely to prison governors, with full government
authority.

5. The Atrocious Dr Edward Trevor

By September of 1798 in the wake of the ineffective rebellion, Charles, First Marquis Cornwallis was settling unhappily into his new position as lord lieutenant. He had been given the dual responsibility because of his past military expertise as commander-in-chief of the armed forces of His Majesty in Ireland, and was soon to be entrusted with the bringing about of an Act of Union between the two kingdoms.[1] The yeomanry in Ireland were numerous and powerful. In the Loughlinstown, Co. Dublin, camp alone there were 1,500 soldiers. According to Cornwallis the yeomanry, who had saved the country from a serious outbreak of rebellion some three months earlier, were now themselves taking the lead in rape and murder.[2]

In the closing months of the eighteenth century Cornwallis was writing to General Ross, Surveyor of His Majesty's Ordnance Survey:

The vilest informers are hunted out from the prisons to attack with the most barefaced perjury the lives of all those who are suspected of being disaffected and indeed every Roman Catholic of influence remains in the greatest of danger.

Behind the high walls of Kilmainham change was also taking place, with the new administration of Edward Trevor. He had come to his new position from the ranks of the army and for several years to come would leave his special mark of cruelty on the life of the prison.

Trevor's ascendency brought about an immediate worsening for the state prisoners.[3] Kilmainham now became the nearest thing to a living hell hole. Edward Trevor was ably supported by his Chief Gaoler, George Dunn. The prisons most recently appointed Keeper, John Dunn, an Englishman with a kind nature was to have all authority immediately removed from him. Trevor instantly took hold of the reins of office, and assumed the role of terrorist and tyrant, making Kilmainham a place of fright and fear, for both prisoners and prison staff alike.

Several documents giving evidence of Trevor's cruelty were smuggled out of the prison.[4] This action on discovery would have resulted in a fate worse than death since every petition going out from the prison had to go through the doctor's hand for censorship. Trevor was effectively able to control the thoughts and words of the prisoners under his charge. On the other hand, he could flavour and favour the petition, with a view to reinforcing his position of strength within the prison. Very many of the prisoners' petitions had in their closing paragraph of submission to the lord lieutenant a glowing account of the newly arrived Trevor, so that his 'kindnesses' were well read within government circles. Only with this mandatory praise of the doctor had the petition of the prisoner a slim chance of seeing the light of day, and arriving at its Dublin Castle destination.

Prisoner James Power was brought to Kilmainham in May 1797 on suspicion of belonging to the outlawed Society of United Irishmen. From his prison cell for the second time on 20 March 1799 he was writing to the lord lieutenant asking to be taken to trial; for two and a half years he had 'languished in one of the dark cells of Kilmainham, under all the rigours of close confinement, without trial or without ever making an appearance in court'.[5] Power went through the official channel of submitting his petition to Edward Trevor, for safe delivery to the lord lieutenant, but his petition was mysteriously lost or mislaid, while Edward Trevor without cause or consultation had him placed upon a prison ship at Waterford, awaiting transportation.

In complete contrast, Thomas Griffith and Thomas Heath, both of His Majesty's armed forces in Ireland, were discharged from Kilmainham Gaol minutes after their arrival there on a charge of being involved in the firing of a pistol at one James Evans. Trevor, himself a justice of the peace, had them brought before a justice and they were given liberty in a matter of minutes following their court appearance. The justice deemed that it appeared clear and evident to the court that the gun in question had discharged itself by accident, and the two yeomen were freed to rejoin their regiment.[6]

Thomas O'Flanagan, a wealthy Dublin pharmacist and graduate of Trinity College, living in Birr, Co. Offaly was writing to the government first secretary Alexander Marsden, in August of 1800 on the subject of his wife's brother, Henry Morres, a state prisoner in Kilmainham Gaol.[7] O'Flanagan was anxious to ease his wife's family distress and to visit his brother-in-law in the hopes of making his confinement easier by the provision of any needs he might have, and to sort out any help or assistance in obtaining counsel.

Permission was granted for the proposed visit by direct order of the lord lieutenant, but the man's journey from Offaly was in vain, since Edward Trevor adamantly refused him admission to the prison, meeting him at the door only to turn him away, in spite of pleadings. Not surprising since his brother-in-law's letter of Christmas Eve of the same year, smuggled safely out of the prison by secret means, reveals that under Doctor Trevor's 'care' he had been languishing for twenty-five months in solitary confinement, completely debilitated in body, and tortured and deranged in mind.[8]

The unfortunate and miserable man in his petition to Dublin Castle was seeking refuge from the torments of melancholy, and an overpowering loneliness following a long isolation. He requested that he might be allowed to associate with some prisoners of his own class during the hour of recreation – he could hear and see them through the narrow grid in his solitary dark cell talking together.

Solitary confinement and all the torturous deprivations that came with the act were Edward Trevor's speciality. He strove to subdue those in his care into a state of total submission until he saw before him a bent and broken man, fit for his own use. His method was more mental than physical and produced many casualties of mind and of body.[9]

The unfortunate prisoner in a solitary cell was deprived entirely of association or even the pleasure of hard physical labour. He was sometimes bound in irons, bringing about a state of complete mental, physical and spiritual wretchedness.

Melancholia and madness were fast becoming the isolated prisoner's closest friends.

Edward Trevor used the provision of putrid animal flesh, served with rotten vegetables, (mostly cabbage) eaten alone in a darkened cell under solitary confinement as the strongest weapon to weaken any resistance to his tyranny.[10] Nobody dared to question or complain of his cruelty as they were certain that things could only get worse, with an added weakening of mind and body on a diet of bread and water. This was the cruellest of punishments, since the solitary cells were situated in the dungeon semi-basement level of the prison, where the prison kitchens were also located. The aroma of food being prepared for prisoners and staff alike was calculated to tantalise an already tortured mind and body.

Trevor's torture was designed to break the strongest body, but not even his barbaric treatment and all its associated deprivations could quench the ideals of some of the men confined in the prison with a thirst for a free and united Ireland.

The doctor allowed state prisoners to eat together in one of the gaol's narrow corridors. However, with the help of certain privileged prisoners – usually felons – Trevor ensured that meal times became a horrifying ordeal. His 'spying workforce' – who were paid in privileges to help further his cruel methods – left slop buckets containing the human waste of the state prisoners in the corridor through which the unfortunate men had to wade on their way to table.

Many of them were deprived of air and of exercise, while James Tandy, son of Napper Tandy, fell victim to Trevor's regime during a rigorous confinement.[11] Lack of accommodation, adequate to cope with the swelling prison population, made it necessary for Tandy to share a cell with four other state prisoners. They were provided with a bucket and were obliged to perform the offices of nature in the presence of each other. At meal times the unemptied bucket was taken out of the room and placed beside the prisoners at table, while on at least one occasion Tandy records that the plates and the cutlery from which they had eaten were washed in the same bucket. When Tandy complained, along with other prisoners including John Palmer, William McDermott, Philip Long and Henry Hughes, Trevor retorted that the prisoners could be assured that he was acting with the full knowledge of the government, and under the express order of the lord lieutenant's office.

Fate was now dealing a cruel hand to Sir Edward Newenham who had so earnestly more than a decade previously striven for the establishment of the New County of Dublin Gaol at Kilmainham.

On the 20 October 1800, Sir Edward Newenham was arrested by four bailiffs and handed over to military custody on the execution of a warrant for the failure of payment on the interest of a debt amounting to £630 and costs, on the recent sale of his Coolock manor home, Belcamp House. He was seized and publicly exhibited through the streets of Dublin in the prison delivery cart, an embarrassing and humiliating experience in the life of one who had been earlier elected to represent the people of Dublin City and County in the House of Parliament. He had now lost not only his parliamentary seat and the immunity and privileges that went with that station, but also his freedom of movement.[12]

Following a brief stop at his lawyer's office, in return for a bribe of four guineas to his military escort, the bankrupt and nervous Newenham was received at Kilmainham in a state of nervous exhaustion, to sample at first hand the hospitality of the prison he had helped to establish.

Kilmainham Gaol from the inside was a very different and frightening experience. The gaol was now bursting with a swelling population of state prisoners, and lacked the space to accommodate its new titled inmate. Sir Edward was placed in a first floor room to the front of the prison, adjoining the gaolers apartment, close to the entrance to the execution plank outside the prison where the execution of Timothy Doolan for the crime of sheep stealing had taken place a few hours earlier.[13]

Edward Newenham's first night behind the high walls of Kilmainham was long and sleepless troubled further by a bad bronchial cough and a high temperature, aggravated by fright and the sparseness of the room which contained no furniture save a mattress on the floor. Gathering all of his reserves of strength, Newenham immediately set about writing a petition to the lord lieutenant seeking respite from the harsh and unfamiliar surroundings of Kilmainham. The eerie sound of the execution plank swaying outside, teased by the October winds, grated upon his shattered nerves.

Newenham's petition was handed directly to the lord lieutenant by Alexander Marsden, the first secretary, who in turn despatched word to the impoverished politician that the government alas could offer no relief in terms of a lighter sentence.[14] However, instructions were sent to Dr Trevor that better accommodation was to be found for him within the prison. He was immediately removed to a room at the rear of the central block, bringing further strain on a troubled prison population, while his family, now living on British charity, tried to raise the money necessary to pay his debt and ultimately secure his release.

Following the passing of the Act of Union between the Kingdoms of Ireland and England, which became law on New Year's Day 1801, the Irish House of Parliament was abolished. As a result of that union the Irish members of the British Parliament were rendered a small ineffective minority, just as Britain's Premier Pitt had planned they should be. The Catholic population of Ireland remained suppressed, increasing in their frustration and anger. There was whispered talk of insurrection.

The opening months of the nineteenth century saw Cornwallis distressed and in a state of restlessness. The watchmen of the city and county of Dublin were adding to his problems, complaining of bad pay and long hours.[15] Cornwallis however found some relief in his personal correspondence, and around this time was writing again to General Ross. He voices his unhappy situation:–

My occupation is now one of the most unpleasant in its nature, negotiating and jobbing with the most corrupt people under heaven. I despise and hate myself every hour for engaging in such dirty work...
The conversations of the principal persons of this country

all tend to encourage the system of blood and the conversation even at my table, where you may suppose I do all I can to prevent it, has always turned to hangings, shootings and burnings. If a priest should be put to death, the greatest joy is expressed by the whole company. Yet the Catholics are expected to roll back the tide of nature and fondly lick the hand that so barbarously beats them.

New plans were afoot, there was fresh unsettled rebellion in the air, and one young patriot was busy with a high and costly ideal of freedom.

His name was Robert Emmet.

6. Robert Emmet and Anne Devlin

Robert Emmet was born in Dublin's Molesworth Street on 4 March 1778, son of an eminent Dublin physician. He was the youngest of eighteen children born to the union of Dr. Robert Emmet and his Kerry born wife, Eileen Mason. Five of these children were named after their father, but none survived infancy. Robert, junior to his brother Thomas Addis Emmet by fourteen years, grew to learn and love the principles of Wolfe Tone, a constant visitor to the Emmet household on Dublin's Stephen's Green.

From Kilmainham Gaol, Thomas Addis Emmet was banished to Scotland and ultimately to the shores of America. Following an extended visit to Europe, during which he sought assistance for his proposed plan of insurrection Robert Emmet returned home to Dublin in March of 1803.[1] More and more Emmet was convinced that a fresh attempt should be made to strike a blow for freedom. The Act of Union was now two and a half years old.

By early April Emmet had negotiated the lease on a house in Butterfield Lane, Rathfarnham, under the assumed name of Ellis.[2] From this base, nestling in the shadow of the Dublin mountains, he set to work on the refinement of his plan to lead an army of Irishmen into battle against British rule. Its close proximity to the home of Sarah Curran, daughter of the noted Defence Counsel John Philpott Curran, and the object of Emmet's affections, enabled the young lovers to share time together following Emmet's long exile.[3]

The house was within a convenient distance of the mountain hide-out of Michael Dwyer who had successfully evaded all attempts at capture for the best part of five years, for his part in the outbreak of 1798. Emmet had been promised help and assistance from him in the furtherance of his plans.[4] To ensure that the house had a perfectly normal outward appearance, Michael Dwyer suggested that his young first cousin, Anne

Devlin, who lived with her family near Rathfarnham, should be asked to take on the position of housekeeper.[5]

Anne Devlin's role was to go much further than maintaining an appearance of normality within the neighbourhood. She was to become an essential support to Emmet, and was privy to all plans and to all plan-making. From time to time Anne ferried notes between Sarah and Robert, and along with Michael Quigley (whom Anne did not like or trust), Thomas Russell and James Hope, took up residence at Butterfield Lane, where the plans for the forthcoming rising were finalised.[6]

Philip Long, a wealthy Dublin merchant gave support and finance.[7] Four buildings were leased with Long's assistance in the vicinity of Dublin's Coombe. Two were never used, one functioned as a storehouse, and the work of pike-making took place in Mass Lane, between Thomas Street and the river Liffey. On the afternoon of 16 July at Mass Lane, an unfortunate and premature explosion took place, damaging morale and resulting in the loss of one life.

Emmet had decided on the evening of Saturday 23 July as the date for the rising. The venture was doomed from the outset. On paper, Emmet's well thought out plan bore all the hallmarks of military brilliance, but the doctor's son was hindered by his own lack of resources and loss of morale among his men, and in particular by his own trusting nature. Emmet expected those who surrounded him to possess the same nobility of mind that he himself had, when in reality he was surrounded by spies and informers.[8]

Dublin Castle was not even reached, Michael Dwyer and his band of men never left their mountain hide-out, while Emmet was finally arrested by the notorious Town Major, Henry Charles Sirr, in Harolds Cross. After extensive questioning in Dublin Castle, Emmet was lodged in Kilmainham Gaol.[9]

Over two hundred special warrants were issued and resulted in arrests on charges relating to the evening of 23 July. Those arrested were imprisoned in Newgate and Kilmainham. These included Philip Long, John Patton, whose sister Jane was married to Thomas Addis Emmet and St John Mason, Emmet's first cousin.[10] Martin Burke of Francis Street was arrested on the information of a woman called Dunn with whom he had a

personal quarrel. Sarah's letters were discovered on Robert
Emmet's person when he was arrested, and another he had
written to her was found at the Mass Lane depot by one of the
military and handed over to Dublin Castle. This above all else
was to cause Emmet distress and concern during his last days in
Kilmainham as Doctor Trevor tried to discover the identity of
the writer.

On the evening of 29 August 1803, Anne Devlin, along with
her parents, brothers and sister, were arrested in Rathfarnham. They were walked to Dublin Castle, a distance of
some ten miles, the men with their hands bound behind them,
their trousers cut from fastenings, so that any movement of the
hands would result in their trousers falling down. After
separation at Dublin Castle and long hours of questioning, Anne
and her brothers and parents, along with her young brother
James aged eight, were given over to Doctor Trevor's custody in
Kilmainham Gaol.[11]

For Anne, this was the beginning of a three year nightmare.

She was not told of Emmet's presence in the prison, and in the
meantime outside the prison walls evidence against him was
being collected on a massive scale to be used at his trial. Mr
Justice Bell, one of the chief magistrates of the county was busy
taking depositions, and several people suspected of being
associated with the events of the night of 23 July were taken
into prison, shown the unfortunate prisoner Emmet and
terrorised into giving evidence against him in return for their
own lives.[12]

Doctor Trevor believed that he could glean information quite
easily from Anne Devlin, and began to work on her
immediately. He started gently at first, but when she refused
to break down under his questioning and offer information
voluntarily, he became extremely agitated and replaced his
former benign approach with his more usual form of sadism.
Town Major Sirr called to the prison, especially to assist in the
questioning of Anne, and warned her that she must tell where
the leaders were if she wanted to save her family. Doctor
Trevor hinted at the awful shame of a public execution.[13]

Day in day out Anne was questioned, bullied, threatened
with certain death, and harangued by the major and the

doctor. She was then in contrast offered a 'Dowry' of £500 in return for any helpful information she might give. But it was to no avail. Anne's will was stronger than all the bullyings, and her dedication to Emmet, and in particular to the cause they stood for, was stronger than anything they could do to her. Major Sirr, in desperation, told her that he would see to it that she spent the remainder of her days in Kilmainham Gaol, while the doctor took his turn further threatening and bullying.

When Anne was admitted to the prison, Doctor Trevor had marked beside her name in the register the two words 'To Prosecute' meaning that she would be called upon to give evidence against Emmet.[14] This was an optimistic entry on the part of Trevor.

On 3 September, Robert Emmet wrote from his cell in Kilmainham to Secretary Wickham asking if he could have free communication with some friends, pleading for the lives of others to be spared, and earnestly beseeching that no harm would come to the person to whom he had written that last letter, and whose letters were found on his person on arrest.

Robert Emmet refused to purchase his own safety, and vowed to stand his trial. He asked that Counsellor Burton, an associate of Sarah's father would be sent to him in Kilmainham so that he could prepare his defence. He was greatly distressed in case Sarah's name might be made public or that any proceedings would be taken against her. He spoke of her only as 'that particular person' and was ready to sacrifice for her any thoughts of his own personal safety. Doctor Trevor however was looking for specific details from Emmet as to the locations of further depots and arms' caches, and insinuated that if this information was forthcoming the government might be prepared to act leniently towards 'that person'.

George Dunn, fast becoming Trevor's most able cohort, was making use of the time that Emmet had to himself in his high security cell, with overtures of friendship which the hapless Emmet believed to be genuine. Encouraging Emmet to use him as a messenger (only so that he could report the proceedings to Doctor Trevor) Dunn brought a letter to Emmet's first cousin, St

John Mason, also a prisoner in Kilmainham, containing the remark that Emmet believed that an offer of money to Dunn might enable an effective escape.[15]

Dunn played along with the plan and reported developments to Trevor. Mason did offer Dunn £500 with the promise of an additional £500 if Emmet's escape from the country was effected. Dunn performed to perfection. Trevor was briefed in great detail on every word. A note passed to Emmet through Dunn from his cousin, was intercepted by Trevor before it arrived to Emmet's cell and a copy was sent to Dublin Castle to be read by Secretary Wickham.

The plan of escape as Robert Emmet saw it was to acquire the key of the prison from John Dunn. The plan of escape was to include four other prisoners, but no specific information is available as to who these were. Emmet did not yet know of Anne's presence in the dungeons.

Emmet's hopes were dashed when Dunn said he could do no more for him. The situation was getting out of hand, and Dunn had been told to step back by Trevor. But Emmet continued to look on Dunn as his friend.

On the afternoon of 8 September, Anne Devlin and Robert Emmet came unexpectedly face to face in one of the yards to the rear of the prison. Trevor was by now obsessed with breaking Anne's will. He went personally to her dungeon one afternoon and asked if she would like to 'take the air'. Anne only wanted to be left alone with her thoughts but the doctor frogmarched her out into the open, pushed her into a yard and slammed the door behind her.

She found herself looking at Robert Emmet, playing with a tennis ball against the prison wall. The slamming of the yard door drew Emmet's attention, and on turning his head, the two friends came face to face with each other – for the last time. Anne made no move to greet him, but frowned hard and looked significantly at the window above the yard from where she knew that Doctor Trevor was keeping an expectant watch.

Robert Emmet manoeuvred the tennis ball in the direction of Anne, so that he could speak with her. Stooping to retrieve it he spoke softly to the girl, urging her to tell what she knew of

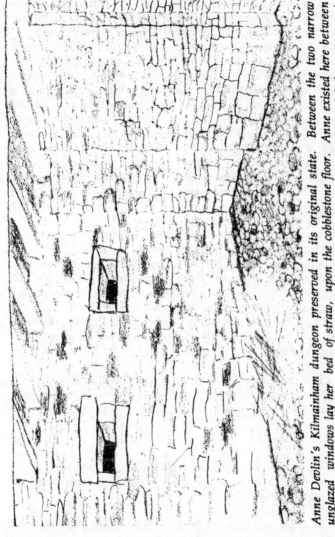

Anne Devlin's Kilmainham dungeon preserved in its original state. Between the two narrow unglazed windows lay her bed of straw, upon the cobblestone floor. Anne existed here between 1803 and 1806, and she was never charged with any crime or never appeared before any court. (Drawing by Martin Crawford.)

him, so that her family could be free. Anne commenced walking the circular exercise path of the prison yard, stopped near to him, stooped to remove a piece of imaginary gravel from her shoes and reprimanded Emmet for thinking that she could even consider giving information against him, and warned him again that Trevor was watching from the window.

Emmet pleaded with her to secure her family's freedom. He knew there would be many to swear evidence against him and said that he would be unable to die easy while she and her family were in such danger. She retorted that not for a thousand pounds, not for the whole world would she swear one syllable against him. Anne continued walking, taking no further notice of Emmet while Trevor's anger from his window look-out reached boiling point. Infuriated by the failure of his plan, he was now more than ever determined to break this wilful Wicklow woman's mind and spirit.[16]

On the morning of 9 September, Robert Emmet's mother died. Word did not reach him in Kilmainham for several days.

Trevor now turned again in earnest to George Dunn for assistance. He wanted to be the one to boast to Dublin Castle that it was through his resources that 'that particular person' as spoken of by Emmet was identified. He sent Dunn to Emmet, offering to take a letter out of the prison for him to anyone he wanted. In all good faith Emmet, from his Kilmainham cell, wrote to Sarah:

> My dearest love. I never felt so oppressed in my whole life as at the cruel injury I have done to you. I was seized and searched before I could destroy your letters....

He concluded:

> I would with joy, lay down my life for you, but ought I do more. I have written in the dark. My dearest Sarah, please forgive me.

Addressing the envelope to *Miss Sarah Curran*, he handed it to George Dunn. Trevor had triumphed at last.

Following Emmet's trial at Green Street courthouse, on 19 September 1803, where he appeared before Lord Justice Norbury on a charge of high treason, and where the Jury found him guilty without one witness being called to speak in his favour. He was sentenced to be publicly executed outside St Catherine's Church, in Thomas Street on the following day.

He was returned late in the night to Kilmainham, and passed his last hours in the room known today within the Gaol as the Robert Emmet Room. At that time it was the office of the Matron.[17] At 1.30 pm on 20 September, the Sheriff of Dublin arrived to escort the prisoner under heavy military guard to the place of execution.

After the execution, Emmet's body was returned to Kilmainham Gaol. It is said that on Doctor Trevor's instructions it was removed from the prison precinct, and buried inside the grounds of the Royal Hospital, in the vicinity known as Bully's Acre. It is further alleged that some days later some of Emmet's friends, on discovering the burial place, came and removed it, but where they took it to or where the body of Emmet now lies, remains a mystery.[18]

Ironically, he did say in his speech from the dock:

> Until my country can take her place among the great nations of the world, let my tomb remain uninscribed, and my body lie somewhere in obscurity.

Emmet's young life was now over. Anne Devlin's three year incarceration was only beginning.

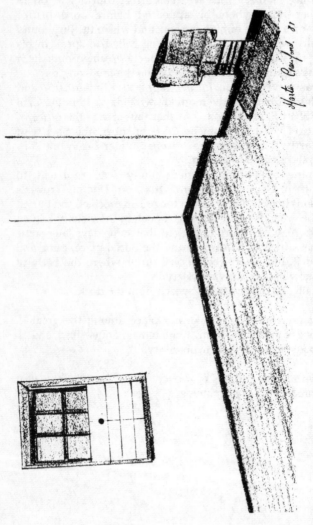

Martin Crawford. 81

The Robert Emmet Room as it is today in Kilmainham. The peep-hole in the boarded section of the window was used as a viewing point for informers brought into the prison for prisoner identification, from 1900 onwards. (Drawing by Martin Crawford.)

7. Fears, Fevers, Floggings

With the disastrous outcome of Robert Emmet's rising, the spirit of rebellion in Ireland had subsided only to come alive again forty years later. Meanwhile the freedom of the notorious Michael Dwyer, Anne Devlin's first cousin, was causing concern to Dublin Castle Officials.[1] Within four months of the numerous September executions, these fears were themselves quenched by Dwyer's induced surrender to the government, commencing with long hours of questioning in Dublin Castle and culminating with his arrival at Kilmainham Gaol in an advanced state of inebriation on Christmas Eve, 1803.[2]

Doctor Trevor immediately began negotiations about conditions for safe passage to America, with Dwyer and those of his men who had earlier surrendered into official custody, but this fell through when the government reneged. Dwyer and his wife and party left Kilmainham Gaol bound for the shores of Botany Bay, on board the *Tellicherry*, in August, 1805.[3]

Anne Devlin was still undergoing the rigours of Doctor Trevor's cruelty within Kilmainham. Her health was now badly impaired, but her spirit never broke. Trevor's treatment of many of the state prisoners, but in particular his treatment of Anne provoked an investigation of conditions within the gaol by the court of the King's Bench. No action resulted following this investigation and astonishingly Trevor's salary was raised to £400 per annum, an increase of almost 100%. This increase endorsed his approved status within government circles.

For the next fifteen years Trevor embarked upon a major economy drive within the prison. He reduced the allowance of every state prisoner from five shillings and five pence per prisoner per day, to three and three pence. He expended only one shilling and seven pence halfpenny on each prisoner, being the official allowance for those prisoners on the felon side of the prison, just enough to scarcely subsist upon.

The diet now required by law to be served to each prisoner within Kilmainham according to a revision of the Act of George III (Cap 74) was one quart of milk, half a pound of bread and five pounds of potatoes daily. Meat, fish or chicken was served only to the prisoners under medical supervision, and on direct orders issued to the keeper by the visiting prison doctor. From 1810 provisions were served to the prisoner in his cell. Kilmainham's diet was distributed twice daily, with breakfast at 8 am and dinner at 2 pm. There was no further meal until the breaking of fast at 8 am the following morning. Dinner was followed by four hours of hard labour.

Taking further steps to find favour with the government, Edward Trevor reminded them in 1808 of his notable public service to the crown in Ireland, while seeking the prestigious and highly paid position of Inspector General of His Majesty's prisons in Ireland. In 1810 Trevor asked for a military guard to be placed on his Fitzgibbon Street home, as he feared his family was in danger.[4] His influence on Kilmainham would be felt even beyond his relocation to Cork in 1817 when he was appointed as inspector of prison ships, with all responsibility for supervising the embarkation of prisoners under sentence of transportation.

The despairing journeys from Kilmainham and other prison depots of those convicts sentenced to banishment dragged on until 1853, as hordes of unfortunates without friend or finance embarked to form the origins of Irish-American and Irish-Australian communities. It was a sentence then as dreadfully feared as the death sentence. Some failed to survive the harrowing sea journeys, while others lost the will to live and hope.

In Kilmainham prisoners existed under crowded and inhumane conditions waiting the readiness of weather and vessels, herded together in an always over-populated side of the prison. The prison ships themselves were dirty, some leaked, all were rat infested, and once on board the prisoners were chained two by two until every available shipboard space was crammed. Some starved to death.[5]

A view of the prison ship from any quayside was heartbreaking, and punctuated with many tearful scenes as members of a family came in great distress to catch a last helpless look at a departing dear one. Christopher Doyle from Dublin was one of those passengers, leaving Kilmainham in 1810, sentenced to transportation for life for stealing iron. His health was so impaired on arrival at Waterford that he was returned to the custody of George Dunn in Kilmainham. He was to stay there for a further twenty-two months before being fortuitously freed by the Honourable H.B. Blackwood, High Sheriff of Dublin, on a visit to the prison.[6]

Daniel Kelly also shared that same journey, having been convicted at the Carrickfergus Summer Assizes of 1808 for stealing a pocket book or wallet. Likewise he was turned around and without delay despatched back to Kilmainham because of an ulcerous and incurable leg. Doctor Trevor wanted to perform an amputation of the diseased limb, but the sick and crippled prisoner was instead isolated in a remote and secure cell in the depths of the prison, where he would have no contact with any other prisoner, in case his leg should infect the gaol population.

David Doyle, from Clonmel, Co. Tipperary, was found guilty of taking arms and ammunition and in the spring of 1810 was too weak to survive a hazardous sea journey aboard a crowded prison ship. He was confined in Kilmainham, deprived of the use of all of his limbs, unable to master movement in any form, even with the assistance of crutches. Finally, George Dunn, possibly because of Doyle's nuisance value urged the government to free him.

By now the staff of Kilmainham had been augmented by the taking on board of George Simpson, formerly a turnkey at the notorious Newgate. Simpson was as infamous as Trevor for his ill-treatment of the prisoners under his care, and on Wednesdays and Fridays, the days set aside specially for 'further punishments', the floggings were carried out, breaking skin with catskin lashes while Simpson ceaselessly tried to break the spirit of the people behind those high Kilmainham walls.

Margaret Scott, a convict from Derry awaiting transportation, broke the routine of an August day in 1810 within the prison, by giving birth to an infant son. It was a

spectacle that stirred momentarily even the hard heart of
Edward Trevor, who had her removed 'on compassionate
grounds' to the penitentiary side of the prison. Here she was
forced to perform domestic chores, but always in the company of
her baby. Her sentence of transportation was commuted on the
intercession of Trevor to the government, and the deed stands
out from Trevor's many cruelties by its singular compassion.[7]

The same month the governors of the House of Industry had
completed a report on a February visit to the gaol, acting on the
instructions of the lord lieutenant, to carry out a feasibility
study on the idea of introducing some form of industrious labour
into the prison.[8] The treadwheel was performing its useless
tiring function daily in all prisons of the era, draining each
prisoner in turn of all physical strength while performing no
useful work. Stonebreaking and oakum picking were the only
forms of work established within the prison system.

The visiting committee reported favourably on the high
sense of security within Kilmainham, but expressed concern
that within the entire internal areas of the gaol there was not
sufficient light in any of the rooms suitable for the purposes of
industry. Their report resulted in several workshops being
established in the yard area of Kilmainham, including a
carpenters shop which would undertake prison maintenance
and repair.

A trickle of transfer traffic passed from Newgate Prison to
Kilmainham, so that young able-bodied prisoners could man
the new workshops. These included two thirteen year old boys
named James Leonard and Terence Hughes, both from Dublin,
along with John McArdle and Peter Farrell. They happily
agreed to perform whatever industrious tasks were asked of
them believing the transfer to be a better method of existence
than their confinement within Newgate had been.[9]

Outside Kilmainham's front doors the continued executions
took their weekly toll in a public fashion. On the afternoon of
26 May 1812, Thomas Bolger had his sentence of death carried
out by public execution.[10] On the evening prior to the execution,
one of his Majesty's prison inspectors visited the gaol to ensure
that all was in readiness for the forthcoming event. At the
appointed hour over one hundred heavily armed military

guards stationed at the Royal Hospital kept the thronging audience at bay.[11]

At the close of 1814, prisoner Thomas Byrne, late of Francis Street, Dublin wrote to the government from his solitary cell in Kilmainham, asking that he might be allowed to take up a position on the convict side of the prison and join the next stream of transports, declaring that life within Kilmainham and all the hardships such close confinement brought with it, no longer had any meaning for him.[12]

On the morning of 24 November 1816, William Harty, state physician to the gaol of Newgate in Dublin's Green Street was called from his home at 32, Gloucester Street, by a messenger bearing the news of an outbreak of fever at the prison. When he arrived at Newgate he found nine prisoners in an advanced stage of fever and set about isolating them from the rest of the prison population. Newgate, however, was full to capacity, and a hurried decision had to be taken by the government to remove some of the unaffected prisoners to Kilmainham.

Back at Kilmainham word filtered through of the outbreak and prisoner transfer. Discipline broke down and verged on riot.

Part of this transfer contingent contained James Smyth, under sentence of death, with a bad record for several times unsuccessfully attempting to make his escape from Newgate. George Dunn secured him in a remote cell within Kilmainham, so that there would be no conspiracies among those prisoners under his charge. Smyth was safely delivered at the appointed date to the gallows at Newgate – the sister gallows of Kilmainham.

Also in the frenzied evacuation of Newgate was prisoner Gerald Hope, who up to the time of his arrest, charged with forging stamps, had been a happily married man and the successful proprietor of a coffee house in Sackville Street (now O'Connell Street). Since his loss of reputation, property and family, his health had deteriorated drastically. To the concern of Doctor Harty his once broad frame was on arrival at Kilmainham, a sickened skeleton. His mind was falling into the realms of madness, and he had already made two foiled attempts on his life, within Newgate, almost succeeding on the

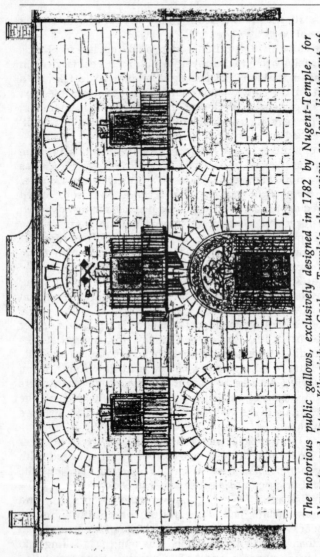

The notorious public gallows, exclusively designed in 1782 by Nugent-Temple, for Newgate and later Kilmainham Gaol. Temple's short reign as lord lieutenant of Ireland lasted a mere seven months. The last public execution was carried out on Kilmainham's gallows in 1860. (Drawing by Martin Crawford.)

last endeavour. He took a quantity of rat poison strong enough in volume to destroy him. His life was saved by the quick thinking of one of the prisoners sharing his room, who forced an amount of whiskey down his throat causing him to vomit. As Hope was sent to recover within the overcrowded infirmary of Newgate his pockets were searched to reveal two letters in his own hand, one requesting to be buried behind prison walls, and the other to his wife bidding her a sorrowful and moving goodbye.

The transfer of Hope to Kilmainham caused the over-worked Doctor Harty great concern as he was suffering from an advanced liver and kidney disease. Merciful approaches were made to the government by Harty to have his sentence of transportation commuted as he was afraid that his patient would not survive the rigours of a long sea journey.

Edward Trevor dashed any prospect of a remission by writing to the lord lieutenant stating that in his medical opinion, notwithstanding any other medical opinion which had been proffered on the subject he believed that 'Hope was shamming'. Hope was now without hope.[13]

By September of 1816 the workshops erected so recently within the prison yards of Kilmainham were idle. It proved more effective for George Dunn to have his charges closely confined and uselessly performing the tedious task of picking oakum behind locked doors in the semi darkness of the cells, or tired wretchedly by the treadwheel.   The Richmond Penitentiary nearby was almost completed and industrious endeavours would be more efficiently carried out there under proper supervision.

On 11 December 1816 George Dunn Keeper of Kilmainham was busy with his own personal worries with the expense of the forthcoming season of presents, peace and goodwill. He had set aside this morning to pay the war office a visit to seek money owed to him for the maintenance of soldiers in the past in Kilmainham.[14] During his absence some of the prisoners managed to break the padlock of a door leading to an unoccupied part of the prison, leading to a roof which would give access to the top of the prison walls, so that they could effect an escape and possibly be home in time for Christmas.

Their plans were foiled and they were caught right in the act by Dunn's return. They spent the festive season in Kilmainham, clapped in heavy irons in a dark punishment cell on a diet of bread and water.

8. Fire and Water

Into Kilmainham Gaol two days before Christmas, 1816, came Catherine Blake and Margaret Matthews, two unfortunate women driven to crime through need and necessity. Margaret Matthews was a widow with three young children, while Blake had also a young family and a crippled husband, unable to provide for their needs.

Both had appeared before the Honourable Justice Torrens earlier in the day, on a charge of stealing fowl, doubtless to provide a fare of some kind for Christmas Day.[1] Both had been sentenced to transportation for seven years. Their pathetic petition to the government in the first days of the new year pleads that they be allowed to undergo sentence of hard labour, however rigorous or long, and thus be enabled to stay in Ireland.

The plight of the women in Kilmainham, caused little concern to the administration there, but within the neighbourhood of the Liberties, where both came from, a great rallying of support was drummed up. They had been prosecuted by Ann Hart and William Moran, of Bridgefoot Street, and attached to their petition were references of good character from Michael Harrington of George's Quay and Robert Moore of Gloucester Street, a neighbour of Doctor Harty's. All pledged support for the women and promised to go security for their future conduct. The petition in the hopeful atmosphere of a new year had the required effect on the lord lieutenant and the women were released having spent a frightening Christmas in Kilmainham.[2]

Within the first months of 1817 the water supply for domestic use in the prison was causing concern. The pump which had specially been put into operation at Islandbridge for the provision of water to both the prison and the Royal Hospital had seized.[3] A visiting trio from the Dublin grand jury came into the prison to inspect the ineffectiveness of the water supply, and voiced concern at its inadequacy. The Dublin grand jury agreed to have the pump replaced. The visiting delegation admired the new tables and forms which had recently been acquired for the prisoners for meals, now communally served in the hall. On the very next day, the same tables and chairs were wrecked in a prison fight.

Some of the prisoners were set to work in the summer months of 1817 repairing flagging in three of the prison yards, while the most significant change in prison life was a change of diet. Potatoes, which up to now had only been served twice a week were substituted for bread at dinner.[4]

On Wednesday 3 December 1817 a serious fire broke out in the old west wing of Kilmainham Gaol.[5] The day had been an especially busy one, for as well as the usual reception of prisoners taken into custody straight from the courts or from one of the city bridewells, there were over 250 convicts ready for despatch in a pre-Christmas clearance of the prison.[6] Gaoler Dunn was away from the prison, escorting several prisoners to Green Street Courthouse, for formal serving of notice of trial on charges meriting the death penalty.

Lock-up had been completed by 4 pm after the prisoners had their last meal of the day at 2 pm followed by an hour's exercise. Everything appeared quiet and in order, and the turnkey was about to relax with a cup of cocoa when flames were suddenly seen shooting up from the roof. The alarm was raised and within minutes every possible assistance had been summoned to Kilmainham. Fire engines from the respective city insurance offices galloped towards the prison, while all available military and police rallied in support. John Alley, the Right Honourable Lord Mayor of Dublin, met with the high sheriff on the way, while word was sent to Gaoler Dunn who set about returning to his burning prison without delay, leaving the prisoners he was escorting in the temporary custody of Newgate.

In the meantime the fire had taken a strong hold on the west wing while firemen amid the confusion and hysterics set about their difficult task of bringing the blaze under control. The task was rendered more difficult by the pressure of need put upon the water pump.

A heavy guard of troops was placed around the exterior of

the prison to prevent any attempt at escape by the inmates, while a close guard was kept especially on the large number of convicts awaiting transportation. The high sheriff gave the orders that the prisoners were to be removed from their cells, and placed in one of the yards. Lord Dunboyne, at the head of a contingent of the 94th Regiment, from nearby Richmond Barracks, assisted with the escort of the prisoners from their cells to the yards.

Outside the prison, there were nearly as many people watching the progress of the fire as would be gathered to witness an execution. There was whispered speculation as to whether the fire had been started by the prisoners deliberately, or if it would destroy the prison completely. The event left the west wing water-damaged and smouldering. There were no major casualties, only two prisoners suffered from fumes. The grand jury held an immediate enquiry into the cause of the fire, chaired by the high sheriff of that year, Sir Comptom Domville. The investigation was satisfied that the fire had been accidental. The chimney stacks were at once rendered useless and unsafe, and tenders invited for immediate repairs and alterations.

The rebuilding of the wing commenced immediately, with some prisoner assistance in the carpenter's shop which was effectively put back into use to cope with this unforeseen circumstance. A number of cells were lost in the rebuilding so that extra space could be provided for the establishment of a work area, fitted with looms. These looms would ceaselessly turn out clothing which in time would clothe the entire prison population of Dublin.

Charles Chetwynd, Earl Talbot, was appointed as lord lieutenant of Ireland on 9 October 1817 and from Kilmainham Gaol convict John Condron wrote to the new first officer of the land seeking mitigation of his sentence of transportation of fourteen years. Without protracted enquires or negotiations Condron was freed. His medical condition within the prison was causing extreme concern, showing all the advanced stages of venereal disease. It was feared that his continued presence in the gaol or on board a prison ship would cause an outbreak of fever.

As George Dunn was preparing to spend the evening of 18 July 1818 at his leisure he was approached by an informer named O'Hara, bearing the news that later the same night the church within the grounds of the Hibernian Military School in the Phoenix Park was to be plundered. Since this was Edward Trevor's Alma Mater, Dunn felt it was almost a personal violation.   Without reporting the matter to the police authorities he believed he had a duty to prevent the robbery, and set out from the prison with a selected support group to lay in waiting for the culprits.[7]

Dunn's watchful vigil paid off. After some hours two men came stealing through the darkness and set about breaking a pane of glass in the church window. Dunn and his party foiled the attempt. The men later identified as Michael McCormick, who it was recorded *'was greatly feared in the neighbourhood of Clonsilla'* and Patrick Morton, were taken back to the prison by Dunn under special escort.[8] The parties came to trial on 31 October, and were sentenced to six months imprisonment. The judge on passing sentence told the defendants that they owed their lives in no small way to Gaoler Dunn and if the attempt had not been foiled the court would certainly be asking for their lives in return.

The County Dublin police authority, however, were not enthusiastic or appreciative of Dunn's attempts. In a statement later sent to the high sheriff they insisted that Dunn, whom they had always found difficult to deal with, should not have taken the matter into his own hands. Dunn was embarrassed by the incident and quickly turned to his strange friend, Edward Trevor for assistance. In the meantime, Dunn had to endure some embarrassing press coverage as two newspaper reports charged Dunn with taking 'Blood money'. Dunn maintained that the bad press coverage was due to a man named Edward Kennedy, formerly a prisoner in the gaol of Kilmainham and later employed by Dunn as a turnkey but eventually sacked. Dunn claimed he had written a number of anonymous letters nurturing his grudge against him.

The newly established Association for the Improvement of Prisons and of Prison Discipline had their headquarters at No. 16, Upper Sackville Street, Dublin. They were anxious to visit

Kilmainham. Their report of 1820 shows that they were well pleased with the system of order and cleanliness within the gaol.[9]

Since 1796 at least four prisoners had been employed on a full time basis whitewashing the walls of the prison. The ceilings of every room and ward were scraped, washed in limestone, and flaked in boiling water and vinegar. The visiting delegation noted:– '...that Kilmainham Gaol may one day become a model for the imitation of other gaols in the kingdom'. The society believed fervently in a regime of hard physical labour, and looked forward to seeing the habits of good industry among those who had held the most wretched positions in society.

Several improvements had also taken place within the yards following the fire in the west wing. Some of them were now paved, some laid with gravel, and a water tap was installed in each of the yards so that the prisoners could do their own washing, and as a further defence against fire.[10]

The sewerage system was beginning to cause some concern to gaoler and prisoners alike. The drains, damaged by wind and weather, were not as effective as they should have been and repairs were made with the assistance of an outside contractor. No prisoners were allowed to participate in this work, since it was feared the proximity of the drains might encourage the digging of an underground tunnel. Not even the gaoler, it seems, realised that the rear wall of Kilmainham Gaol, nearest to the river Camac, goes fifty feet underground until it reaches a final base two feet below the river. This was the most effective means of deterring underground escape.[11]

On a second visit to Kilmainham the Association for Prison Discipline and Reform were not concerned to find that the cell windows within the gaol were unglazed. They noted 'it should be of no concern or consequence to the prisoner who is provided with a blanket under which to sleep, and should not suffer from the cold on this account.' The plank beds had now been substituted for a mattress filled with straw. The latter was changed once a month by necessity, and 'oftener if required'. There were three prisoners to each cell, with the size of each mattress being 2'2".

George Dunn's salary was now £200 per annum while there

were four turnkeys employed, one on a salary of £80 per year and the other three being paid £52 each, yearly.[12]

9. Revision and Reform

Dublin's Pro-Cathedral had been established in 1815, behind the city's main thoroughfare in Marlborough Street.[1] Originally planned to occupy a site of some prominence on Sackville Street, Protestant opposition prevented such a blatant Catholic stance. Since the work was the only achievement of the amateur architect, John Sweetman, the matter was not contested as Sweetman had neither the confidence nor the track record to challenge the opposition effectively. By 1821 Catholic Emancipation was still some distance down the road.

With very great deliberation throughout the rest of the country, religious orders were expanding forcefully, and in Dublin in the spring of 1819 the Irish Sisters of Charity founded their Stanhope Street convent, between the North Circular Road at the Phoenix Park and the River Liffey, on the quays – a distance in all of some two miles from the district and gaol of Kilmainham.[2] Mary Aikenhead, the Cork born foundress of the order, was supervising some interior decoration within the convent on a spring morning in 1821 when a message came to her personally from George Dunn, Gaoler of Kilmainham, seeking her help.[3]

Into his custody had come two teenage girls following a double trial, and both were sentenced to death by public execution on the Kilmainham gallows for murder. Thrown into the bowels of Kilmainham in isolated and solitary confinement, the two girls, both named Bridget were terrified by the prospect of their forthcoming ordeal.[4] Their cries of remorse and terror rose high above the chorus of pain and distemper continuously resounding throughout the prison. This caused considerable concern to Gaoler Dunn and staff and prisoners alike. It seemed that nothing would console them although Dunn did spend time and effort in trying to bring about calm. Refusal to appeal their sentence further anguished the two hapless helpless women.

In response to Gaoler Dunn's call for assistance, Mother Mary Aikenhead entered the confines of Kilmainham Prison for the very first time on 16 May 1821 with a sister companion.[5] They were immediately taken to Gaoler Dunn, and then to visit the unfortunate girls, who at first did not want to talk to anyone. But the sisters persevered and remained with them over the next few days administering calmness of spirit and providing some little ease within the minds of the two teenagers. Through the kindness and patience and constant presence of the two nuns, the girls faced their ordeal calmly and on the afternoon of 21 May 1821, were executed.[6] The sisters went with both of them as far as the entrance to the pinioning room situated behind the middle front first floor window of the prison.

The marks of where the 'Drop' was situated can be clearly seen by the visitor to Kilmainham today, above the entrance.

As both girls stepped out through the window, their last earthly sight was a massive gathering of over five thousand faces of the citizens of Dublin, who had gathered outside the prison to view the afternoon performance.[7] The North and South Circular Roads were buzzing with the event in the hours following the execution, while Mother Mary Aikenhead and her sister companion remained at prayer in the prison chapel, praying for the two Bridgets, as they had promised.

Gaoler Dunn's call for assistance had an immense significance on the future working life of the Irish Sisters of Charity, since it was this call to Mother Mary Aikenhead which decided the foundress to include prison visitation and care of prisoners as part of the work of her growing order in Ireland.[8] Some years later, five Irish Sisters of Charity would set out as the first emissaries of their order, to care for and work with the convicts established in the penal colonies of Australia.

Exactly one week after the double execution an act passed through parliament which made more provision for the establishment of asylums for the lunatic poor, and for the custody of insane persons charged with offences in Ireland only.

It empowered the lord lieutenant to direct any number of asylums for Irish lunatics to be established in several districts, while the grand jury of each county were to provide such sums necessary for the required lands and materials in compliance with the act.[9] Up to now the unfortunates of Dublin Society acquitted of crimes before the courts on the grounds of insanity were lodged within the confines of gaol.

By October of 1822 the Association for the Improvement of Prisons and of Prison Discipline were forcing through changes in regard to the drastic over-crowded conditions in the prisons of the city and county of Dublin. Newgate in that month had 316 prisoners far in excess of what it had been built for, and a section of cellular space on the first floor remained constantly empty to save the gaoler and his staff the bother of cleaning and maintenance.[10] In contrast, every available space within Kilmainham at the same period was densely over-crowded. The Report of the Inspectors General of Prisons for County Dublin in 1823 bears this out. It submitted to the government an urgent recommendation that more gaol accommodation would have to be provided 'as a matter of urgency' for the capital city. An interim suggestion that some of the convict population awaiting transportation from the confines of Kilmainham should be temporarily relocated to another prison gained no acceptance.[11]

From time to time suggestions for better prison conditions were submitted to government circles by a minority who knew of the conditions within the prisons of Ireland. Other benevolent minds gave the matter consideration during evenings at home, or visiting friends, but the matter remained largely a subject of well-meaning conversation in the genteel houses. In a written submission to Government, Robert Croker, Medical Doctor, from his residence at Lisnabrin House, Tallow, Co. Cork, stated that many daily deficiencies could be eliminated by a fresh look at the manner of surveillance of the prisoner. He proffered helpful hints on food and the medical duties of the prison doctor under existing legislation. Doctor Croker had for some time worked in Scotland where he ministered to prisoners there.[12]

At the commencement of 1823, a new treadwheel was

established within Kilmainham for the fatigue and further purposeless occupation of up to 150 prisoners per day.[13] The new advancement in nineteenth century technology was the brainchild of William Cubitt, whose invention occupied practically every county gaol within the kingdoms for over fifty years. The exertions it caused were so rigorous that prisoners were allowed to rest after ten minutes, occupying the next ten minutes in picking oakum seated on a bench beside the

Martin Crawford's reproduction of the Cubitt Treadwheel which at the height of its popularity from 1822 until 1872 was a feature in every county gaol in Ireland and England. The Kilmainham wheel could effectively fatigue up to 150 prisoners per day with its ceaseless, useless purpose.

wheel. This fruitless rota went on for two hours.

By 1824 the grand jury of the county of Dublin were in the process of seeking the benevolent services of a schoolmaster for the gaol of Kilmainham.[14] Their task was made difficult, in the words of J. Finlay, Esq., chairman of the Kilmainham gaol discipline committee, by the fact that the distance of the gaol from Dublin City 'made the obtainment of a gratuitous teacher impossible.'

Further pressure was being put upon the administration in relation to Kilmainham Gaol by an active Visiting Ladies Committee. Morale in the female section of the prison soared high in 1824 when they successfully negotiated the removal of a gruesome structure from the women's exercise yard in which the hangman resided when in attendance.[15] This done, the Ladies set about pushing for the employment of an assistant matron, and succeeded in the introduction of an unwritten rule into the prison, that no male turnkey had access on any business whatsoever to the female accommodation within the gaol.

Also in the prison was young Miss Catherine Nugent, only daughter of a wealthy widow, who resided at 114 Abbey Street, Dublin, confined for the illicit possession of a gentleman's watch.[16] Her plight was worsened in that at the time of the girl's trial the Counsel employed to submit a defence on her behalf failed to make his appearance in court until after sentence had been passed. In his absence his client received a sentence of seven years transportation.

In August 1827 William Keegan, a sickly sixty year old man left his Ballyfermot home in good spirits to sell a cow at Smithfield Market. He had found a buyer for his beast, and good company to share his fortune. Possibly drawn on by the carnival atmosphere of market day, he adjourned to a nearby public house where in his own words he 'began to drink incautiously in the same place for three days.'[17] In a deranged state of mind he staggered into another public house near Kilmainham gaol on his journey home. There Keegan was found to have in his possession a forged note against the Bank of Ireland. Following a harrowing trial and lucky escape with his life, Keegan received a sentence of transportation for fourteen years. He petitioned the government for clemency on

27 October 1827, but by the time his petition came to castle attention, he was already aboard a transportation tender at Kingstown.

Newgate prison was fast declining into a derelict state from its constant overuse and swollen population. The atrocities of prison life were causing concern to the reigning monarch, still deeply agitated by the unsettled question of 'The Catholic Problem' in Ireland. The Prisons Act brought through Parliament on 31 May 1826, provided for the setting up of an Official Visiting Board of Superintendents for the prisons of Ireland, with full authority to visit and examine these gruesome buildings, and to inquire into the conduct of the officers employed in their administration. It reviewed the classification of prisoners, the establishment of proper and distinct apartments, yards and other accommodations in the hope of establishing good order and discipline. Serious consideration was to be given to sanitary requirements, while the act specified that separate cells were to be provided when space within the prison allowed, but in the event of unavoidable crowding, one, or three (but never two) prisoners should be lodged in a cellular confinement together. This is still the custom in prisons today.[18]

The act specifically stipulated that the gaols of Dublin city and county were to be provided with further additions and if necessary, in excess of all others furnished by this law. It also became an offence within the terms of the act to interfere with the conveyance of water pipes to any county prison, proving that the citizens of the district of Kilmainham had indeed been wise in their earlier silence! The administrative charge of the major prisons was vested in the newly created position of governor.

George Dunn became Kilmainham's first governor, and his appointed Deputy was one Edward Allison.[19] From now on, yearly returns of expenditure were to be made to the lord lieutenant. The salary of prison chaplains was set at 'not less than thirty pounds and not more than one hundred pounds in Dublin City and County.'

The fact that space was officially set aside within Kilmainham for the safe custody of persons about to give evidence on behalf of the crown is borne out in a letter from John Clarke, Governor of Maryboro Prison (now Portlaoise), on 28 September 1828 when he is found petitioning the government for remittance of his expenses amounting in all to £3 in transmitting two female crown witnesses, Honor Bale and Mary Gore, for safe custody to Kilmainham.[20]

Traffic to Kilmainham from the over-crowded Newgate remained high, swelled with the overflow of the county's vagrants and paupers from the city bridewells. Most likely because of this, a very heavy and severe bout of itch broke out in Kilmainham in the latter end of 1828 causing concern to Governor Dunn, and discomfort to the great number of prisoners who became affected. The incident brought prison discipline close to riot.[21]

Every prisoner within the gaol as a matter of precaution was washed in soap and hot water, and then laced down with disinfectant; hair was cut, heads were shaved, while prisoners' clothes were burned in one of the prison ovens. Prisoners were then set to work meticulously washing down the walls of the prison interior with hot water and vinegar, while a work party of selected healthy prisoners followed close behind equipped with whitewash buckets and brushes.

Governor Dunn by 1829 had officially adopted the procedure of removing a prisoner's clothes on entry, while a regulation set of prison apparel weaved on the gaol's loom were issued. The prisoner's clothing was then boiled, fumigated, labelled, marked, and set aside in a storeroom until needed for an impending court appearance or on release. By now women prisoners were catering for the clothing needs of the rest of the prison, while also undertaking the washing, ironing and mending. Female prisoners wore check frocks, coloured according to their classification while all prisoners were issued with shoes but not socks.

At the beginning of 1830 the prison boasted of sixty-six separate cells, while the Visiting Inspector, aware of the fragility of order within the prison, was urging the Dublin grand jury to provide thirty-four more cells so that the good order and discipline necessary for effective control would be enhanced.[22]

Kilmainham, like other county gaols was now catering for the reception of military prisoners, who, since the abolition of corporal punishment within the ranks of the army were thrown into the nearest gaol.

10. The 1830s and 1840s

By 1830 Kilmainham Gaol was dilapidated in structure, and severely overpopulated, while no structural changes of any consequence had taken place. The cost of repairs to the prison in the first five years of the new decade amounted to a mere £119-10-5d.[1]

On 2 January 1830 a new Gaol Register was opened. The first entry it contains is on a fifteen year old boy, Joseph Dolan, from Ballyfermot, sentenced to one month in a darkened cell, on a diet of bread and water.[2] For the duration of his confinement he was to be taken out to the yards of the prison on every Friday morning, and whipped. His notorious crime was that he had cut off the tail of a calf!

Throughout the next eighteen years the nature of committals changed radically, reflecting cataclysmic changes in Irish society in general.[3] By 1832 one-fifth of the entire population of Ireland was unemployed and the pangs of hunger were present.[4] The following year the lack of 'a good potatoe supply' forced the gaol diet in Kilmainham back to one of oats, for a number of weeks – an ominous sign from behind those high walls of more than a decade of devastation ahead.[5]

From the passing on the Prisons Act of 1826, life within the gaols of Ireland became more and more uniform. It brought a great order in the regime to know that at the very same hour of every day the same useless labours were taking place behind prison walls. Within every gaol in Ireland meals were taken at the same time, while the hours of prayer, visitation, work and recreation were synchronised by the stroke of a clock, and the turning of a key, following the ringing of a bell.

The two inspectors general of prisons with responsibility for forty-two of Ireland's prisons, including Kilmainham, were expressing solemn anxiety in their written reports to the government. They were concerned that with such poverty outside of prison walls, Kilmainham and other gaols might prove an attractive sanctuary from destitution. In normal times the harshness of prison life operated as a deterrent but in times of general hunger and want they offered the bare necessities of life, food and shelter.[6] Throughout the west of Ireland poverty was overwhelming. There was hardly a family in Mayo or Galway whose breadwinner could gain employment of any sort. The inspectors general were urging the erection of a county gaol in Mayo, acknowledging the signs of unrest fast approaching caused by starvation and a sense of worthless worklessness.

By 1834 the gaol of Kilmainham had four turnkeys. From this time onwards there is a notable increase of ex-military men entering the prison service. They were considered an asset to the enforcement of discipline, and by their army training were thought to be emissaries of well ordered working lives. Under the provisions of the recent act thirty prisoners were issued to the care of one turnkey. The average daily intake to the gaol that year was 93 prisoners per day.[7] Notwithstanding the numbers, each turnkey in Kilmainham had his own area of responsibility, based on prisoner classification. Each turnkey looked after a separate part of the prison. They were all considered equal in rank, their duties being similar but distinct. All were provided with uniforms and all lived within the prison. Their relationship with the prisoners was carefully dictated to by rules drawn up by the local magistrates. They were forbidden to hold any unnecessary conversation with their charges and should give only the necessary commands and relieve whatever wants the prisoners had in as few words as possible.

Newcomers served the first one-third of their sentence under the strictest principles of separation, hard labour and discipline, producing a submissiveness of spirit and bodily fatigue. Classification also became uniform. At Kilmainham until the end of 1848 it would remain :

Total separation of male and female prisoners.
*Male Prisoners under sentence of death.
*Male Misdemeanants convicted but not sentenced to hard labour.

*Male Misdemeanants who maintained themselves.
*Males for trial for felonies not being capital charges.
*Males for trial for capital felonies.
*Male recommittals.
*Males for trial for misdemeanours.
*Males confined for unnatural crimes.
*Male deserters from the army and navy.
*Those giving evidence for the crown.
*Juveniles for trial.

Master debtors for the time being were allowed rooms of superior accommodation, while the poor or pauper prisoner in Kilmainham was forbidden to receive any food, except the allowance of the gaol.[8] He was forbidden to receive any privileges and he was to replace by his labour the cost of his keep within the prison. He suffered constant restraint and discipline and deprived of his liberty was in a general state of degradation and disgrace.

Discipline within the female section had notably improved over recent years. The Hibernian Ladies Society for promoting the improvement of female prisoners, reported frequently to the inspectors general: 'Generally speaking the female prisoners in Kilmainham conduct themselves well. They have made some advance in reading and in spelling.' Female classification within the gaol was by behaviour rather than by offence. The 'lower' classes were always to be placed together, along with women of 'immodest character' and women who had children in gaol, unless a separate room could be found for them.

Bathing facilities close to each classification area were available and used, while a separate infirmary space within the main building was set aside for both sexes. Under an act of parliament this would soon be occupied by helpless lunatics.

A book of 'observations' was to be kept in the office of the gaol in which general daily prisoner behaviour was recorded. The chaplain and visiting doctor kept a similar journal. A visitors' book was also maintained 'with earnest vigilance.'

By 1835 a school had been established within the prison. The turnkeys doubled as schoolmasters, teaching whatever they knew of trade or learning. One of them obviously had

Irish, as the Irish language was being taught in Kilmainham, with 'great zeal' according to the inspectors general in their annual report of that year.

In 1837 the Young Queen Victoria ascended to the throne in England. On 23 December of that year, parliament passed an act to regulate the expense of prison officials' in transmitting prisoners from one gaol to another.[9]

The condition of the country worsened. The Poor Laws of Ireland were introduced in 1838 four years behind those of Britain. The establishment of workhouses throughout the land provided a minute scale of employment for a nation starving and weakened by debilitation. By dusk and by daylight, the spirit of outrage was courting crime. By June of 1838 Kilmainham, Newgate and every available prison space were over-crowded with a despairing and ailing population.

Parliament was making provision for Ireland with the passing of an act 'to make more effectual provisions for the prevention of offences by insane persons *IN IRELAND*'. This made more pressing demands on Kilmainham's over-used confines. It made specific provision for any person discovered in Ireland labouring under circumstances considered to be a derangement of mind, to be indicted, brought before two justices of the peace and lodged within the county gaol 'in strict custody'.[10] The county magistrate decided and declared the sanity or lack of sanity of the citizen appearing before him!

In the meantime those dismal transportation vessels ferried back and forth with a cargo of Irishmen and Irishwomen. The lord lieutenant retained plenipotentiary powers to exercise mercy on any person sentenced to transportation and to allow them to be removed to a lunatic asylum instead. Madness brought on by hunger was the order of the day.

In 1840 Kilmainham continued to cater for the miseries of life. Countless numbers were now being incarcerated for 'Potatoe Stealing' or the 'Stealing of Fowl'.

Early in 1841 Governor Dunn died, four years after Edward Trevor. He was replaced by his Deputy Robert Allison.[11] Kilmainham was entering a new era of administration.

By 1842 parliament passed an act for consolidating the Four Courts Prison, in Dublin, as the only prison authorised to confine the ever increasing number of county debtors. Those confined for debts of under £10 had to be subsided by their creditors in prison, to the sum of two shillings and six pence per week.[12]

At the commencement of 1845 the Kilmainham diet was once again altered to oats, being very nearly always of bad quality, and requiring to be boiled first overnight in water, and then at least twice more. In some prisons this diet was thickened with mice droppings, while every unfortunate who survived outside sought shelter and food within the confines of the prison.

The next two years was to bring devastation and death by famine with the failure of the potato crop in 1845 and again in 1846. During those bad times 390 citizens of Dublin obtained work on the reconstruction of the road to Navan, Co. Meath, through Ashtown, Blanchardstown and Dunshaughlin, and in repairing the coast road to Dun Laoghaire from Blackrock, at a wage of one shilling and eight pence weekly.[13]

On 20 December 1847 the year of O'Connell's death, an act was rushed through parliament at Westminster to 'Prevent Further Crime and Outrage in Ireland', acknowledging the presence of massive unrest.[14] This gave the lord lieutenant the necessary powers to increase the constabulary force and advertised heavy penalties of up to two years imprisonment for those caught bearing unlicensed arms.

The poet Thomas Davis had taken a leading role amongst those people impatient with Daniel O'Connell's constitutional approach. A rebellion in 1848 known as the Young Irelanders' Rising, had little effect. The population was weakened by famine, unwilling and unable to rise, and those concerned including William Smith O'Brien, Terence Bellew McManus, John Blake Dillon, Thomas Francis Meagher, and many others were quickly apprehended, banished by transportation, or given stiff prison sentences. One of its leaders was William Smith O'Brien and since O'Brien addressed a monster meeting at Conciliation Hall, Dublin his commitment to repeal was untiring. His personality was a mixture of eloquence, energy and love of country. Born in County Clare less than one month after Robert Emmet's execution in 1803, he was the second son of Sir Edward O'Brien. He entered parliament in 1826 urged on by a determination to prevent the return of Daniel O'Connell at the Clare elections.

Tried before a special commission at Clonmel for high treason on Thursday, 28 September 1848, he was lodged in Newgate Prison, Dublin, and later transferred to Kilmainham from where he commenced his journey of transportation, leaving Kingstown on the brig *Swift*. Along with him from Kilmainham went Thomas Francis Meagher, Terence Bellew McManus, and many others.

It is popularly believed within Kilmainham today that the infant son of William Smith O'Brien was christened in the Protestant church of the gaol, and only recently a bible bearing the signature William Smith O'Brien was found by one of the guides.[15]

During 1848 Kilmainham Gaol had an average daily intake of approximately 205 prisoners.[16]

The passageway from outer to inner hall. Up to 1850 this was on a level two steps below the outer hall level. Following an accident, a visiting inspector sustained an ankle injury and ordered the passage sloped. The work was carried out by prisoners. (Drawing by Martin Crawford.)

11. Enlargement and Separation

In August of 1849 Queen Victoria visited Ireland with her husband and young family. She sent word ahead of their arrival that if the country had a purse, it should be spent on Her Majesty's poor subjects. Instead there was an array of illuminations to greet the entourage, while Dublin Castle busied itself in royal plumbing operations, installing a special hot water bath for royal use, complete with thermometer.[1] She visited the Royal Hospital, Kilmainham, showing her delight at seeing her royal pensioners 'Looking so Well'.

Over the roadway, within Kilmainham Gaol the harshness of life had taken its toll on a crowded gaol population. During the winter months that followed ten deaths occurred within the prison. Three were pauper prisoners, unwilling and unable to hold fast to the spirit of life in the aftermath of the fatal and devastating effects of widespread famine. One elderly lunatic worried his life away, and six miserable convicts died of nervous anxiety, at the impending horrors of transportation.[2]

Prison discipline was now at its worst. Even though the precinct had gained an additional 22 cells, conditions for the female prisoners had worsened.[3] Structurally the female cell accommodation was seriously defective and the number of admissions was high – approximately forty-eight females a day on charges ranging from the concealment of a birth of a child to prostitution. Astonishingly the number of females admitted on charges of being drunk and disorderly far out-numbered their male counter-parts.[4]

By the beginning of the 1850s Governor Allison's health was failing and he found it necessary to obtain a leave of absence from his working environment. During his absence discipline in the prison, not surprisingly, broke down altogether and Thomas Ward, one of the second class turnkeys was proving particularly lax in the administration of his duties. He allowed visitors into the prison at unorthodox hours to see friends and relatives under circumstances of great informality.[5]

Making an unscheduled and unannounced inspection of the prison during the governor's absence, a visiting inspector found a female visitor and two prisoners huddled together in one of the day rooms over a fire, and sharing a bottle of whiskey between them. 'There were signs of the female visitor appearing very drunk, and the other two were not quite sober' the inspector recorded in his report. Thomas Ward was instantly dismissed for a serious breach of prison rules.

By 1855 a large and ominous crack had appeared in the north-east corner of the boundary wall near the courthouse. The remainder of the wall in several vulnerable parts was sometimes crumbling and all the time weakening. Bearing in mind the seriousness of this situation, and always fearful of an escape attempt proving successful, the board of superintendents had a survey carried out. This revealed that repairing the damage would cost in excess of £1,000 and it was decided that repairs could not be undertaken without major rebuilding.

The inspectors general in their yearly reports had been advocating the rebuilding of Kilmainham for many years. In the first months of 1857 the grand jury of Dublin county finally passed the following resolution – 'that the grand jury is fully of the opinion that an extension and an improvement of the county gaol is absolutely necessary in order to increase the separate accommodation system.' Doubtless this decision was taken following an incident in the early days of January of that year when a prisoner – a convicted arsonist – methodically and very thoroughly set fire to all of the beds and bedding in the part of the prison where he was serving his own sentence. Swift action on the part of prison staff and several prisoners prevented the blaze from taking a grip on the building.[6]

More than a decade previously London's Pentonville Prison had been established on the Caledonian Road, gaining the eye and attention of every architect interested in penal design. Known as 'the model prison', it was designed by Joshua Jebb, and had taken on all the attendant curiosity of a national monument. The King of Prussia had been taken to visit its complicated interior and the husband of Queen Victoria, Prince

Albert, along with the prison commissioners of more than twelve European governments had received a grand tour.[7]

Every detail of London's Pentonville had been meticulously planned. It filled a six and a quarter acre site containing over 500 cells, at a cost of £82,000. Its main attraction was its array of cells, three storeys high, contained within a barrel shaped vaulted space, lined on either side with a network of iron galleries and catwalks. The over-all view from the hall demonstrated an ordered vista of salubrious space showing separate confinement from outside of the cell door without the visibility of the human form cornered in the wretchedness of isolation.[8] Halfway through the 1850s over fifty prisons had been modelled on this panoptic persuasion and the design dominated prison architecture for the next fifty years.

In the Summer of 1857 the Board of Superintendents in conjunction with the grand jury of Dublin announced a competition in which architects were invited to submit plans and estimates for the redesign of Kilmainham Gaol offering a first prize of £25, a second prize of £15 and £10 for the third most acceptable entry. Several suitable entries were received, the first and most satisfactory plan coming from the drawing board of a 34 year old Dubliner, John McCurdy. It was enthusiastically received with its panoptic design and approved of by the grand jury of Dublin, and given the personal sanction of George William Frederick, lord lieutenant of Ireland.[9]

John McCurdy was born in Dublin in 1823. He was ambitious, had an impeccable track record, became the architect to the Board of Trinity College, Dublin, where he carried out the design for the Anatomical Museum, and he laid out the system of drainage in College Park. McCurdy was the commissioned architect to the Benchers of the King's Inn, and designed many existing buildings within the city of Dublin, including the present Shelbourne Hotel and the Royal Marine Hotel, in Dun Laoghaire. He was responsible for the designs of the prisons of Tralee, Co. Kerry and of Naas, Co. Kildare, while he won professional acclaim by public competition for his design of Monaghan and Cavan Asylums.[10]

Finally, after fifty-three years the trafficking of the transportation ships ceased in 1853 providing McCurdy with a large

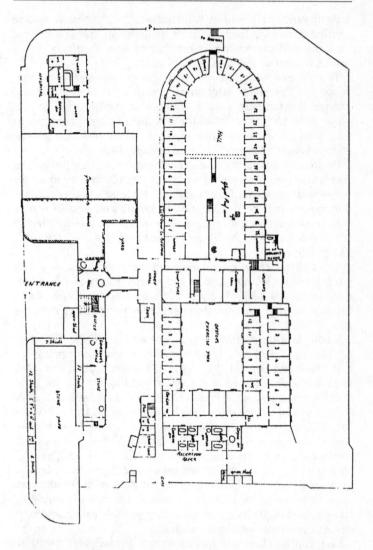

John McCurdy's enlargement plan for the redesign of Kilmainham Gaol (Drawing by Martin Crawford).

area of yard space within Kilmainham.[11] It had been used to confine convict prisoners under sentence of transportation. Parliament declared it feasible that prisons should be lit by artificial means. Kilmainham opted for gas.[12]

The old east wing of the prison was demolished, providing scope for the major alterations. It was the last structural change Kilmainham would undergo in its life as a prison, while John McCurdy, in addition to his £25 prize money was paid £865 for works and design, a cost which included materials and labour all to be completed by May, 1863.

Before any rebuilding could commence the authorities had to take a decision on whether or not Kilmainham was to adopt the separate system of confinement. Howard's earlier separation system had been designed to isolate and punish rather than to pursue the reformation of character. It was decided to adopt the Separate Cell System in as far as it was practicable, and possible.

To facilitate rebuilding, prisoners were removed in small numbers from Kilmainham to the nearby Richmond Penitentiary or to the new Mountjoy Convict Depot on the North Circular Road.[13] All female prisoners were transferred to the gaol of Naas.

School facilities within the gaol ceased during the period of rebuilding. Some experienced tradesmen who were prisoners and who could be trusted to work well under supervision were used in the final stages of carpentry and flag-laying, but only after the boundary walls had been reinforced and strengthened.

The work of demolishing the old east wing began in November 1857 while provision was made at basement level for extended kitchen, bath and laundry facilities.

When the new east wing was completed in 1864, slightly behind schedule it boasted of 101 separate cells on three levels, each specifically designed to receive a portion of sunshine at some time during the day. The window, a fixture in every cell, was situated high enough to make it impossible to see anything other than a patch of sky through it.

Each cell window was glazed with a lifeless piece of glass. None of the windows opened and all were fitted with bars on the outside reducing natural light. Ventilation to each cell came from a duct at the side of the cell door, furnishing each cell at fixed intervals throughout the day with an intake of warm air, drawn in by convector from the basement level of the prison. Foul air was released by means of a fluted vent on the window wall of the cell while large circular stoppers were positioned at strategic intervals on the ground floor. These were from time to time raised to allow a draft of warm air to circulate from the furnace area in the basement of the prison.

In accordance with the character of confinement, each cell door was narrow and low, made of timber reinforced with steel studs. Each had a spyhole (sometimes called the Judas) so that the prisoner could be observed. Each cell door also contained a trap hatch which when released by a key from the outside fell into the position of a tray for the reception of food, delivered twice daily by the warders with all the precision of a military exercise.

When it was time to eat, the prison bell tolled. Immediately from the kitchen area in the basement a tray of bread and large cans of cocoa were raised by means of the food hoist. Two warders passed along each wing on each floor, serving their charges. For the prisoners of course it was the most pleasurable time of the day. Dinner was now served at 3.00 pm and it contained potatoes three times a week. The entire operation took less than ten minutes during which no words were spoken to the prisoners.

Bells were fitted into each cell in the new east wing, since parliament required that every prisoner in separate confinement should have access to a warder at all times of the day or night, in case of sickness or if assistance was needed. At the end of each level were two washrooms and prisoners were let out first thing in the morning in batches of three to empty chamber pots and have a supervised morning wash.

At lock up times each prisoner was carefully checked by means of the spy hole.[14] In many prisons part of an officer's uniform consisted of at least one pair of felt slippers so that he could glide noiselessly along his rounds. But Kilmainham Gaol had its own very definite smell. The seasoned prisoner could sense the approach of a soft-footed warder by the scent of hair oil or shaving lotion. Uniforms and body odours signalled

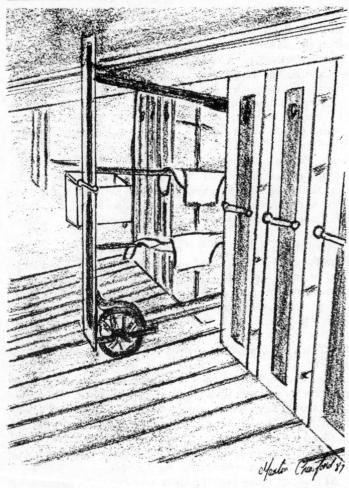

Martin Crawford's impression of the Kilmainham Gaol ground floor laundry as it would have looked, following the completion of the new east wing (circa. 1870). Detail provided by a visit to Mountjoy Prison, courtesy of John Lonergan, Governor. Both laundries are approximately the same age. Note the hot water drying pipes.

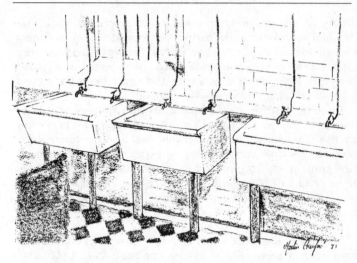

silent approaches.

In the new east wing each prisoner's cell door declared his number and sentence (never his name) identified by a classification prefix number. This number was also duplicated on his prison clothing. No prison officer was to address a prisoner by name. During the recreation hour, the prisoners' faces were covered by a mask of brown cloth with two slits for the eyes. These masks were nearly always manufactured in the prison by the women prisoners. Its purpose was to guard against the danger of collusion or conspiracy, and to protect each prisoner from the threat of blackmail following his release.[15]

The stalls in the Catholic chapel had now been removed. Balcony accommodation provided the church with a second storey, where the women prisoners and off-duty warders attended mass. Previously the prisoners had been isolated in the church within wooden stalls, open at the top, through which they could see the figure of the priest on the altar, but never the prisoner in the next stall. Entry into the church involved a rigorous routine, prisoners filing in three or six at a time, each into his own stall space, never allowed to raise his head, or look right or left. After each prisoner entered he closed his stall latch. When the last stall had been closed a handle at the end of the row was pulled to lock the whole line of box-like cubicles. Following the reconstruction prisoners eagerly looked forward to the church services where the only close contact of prison life took place. Interspersed throughout the seats were warders, while two armed officers took their place at the altar and door, ever vigilant.

To complete the refurbishment an iron railings was later erected at the front of the prison. Kilmainham Gaol now took on the character of an impregnable Bastille. Governor Price invested his time and engineering expertise into designing a new crank pump, to provide hard physical labour for the long-term prisoner. Two large yardspaces on either side of the original central building were added for increased work and recreation space.[16]

The time of the Fenians had arrived. The sparks of 1848 had been kindled anew. For many years preparation and planning had been under way to erupt in open rebellion in 1867.

12. The Fenians

The Fenian Movement was founded on the principles of
Theobald Wolfe Tone – its objectives being to break the connection with England once and for all.[1]

For an organisation which was bound to secrecy the Movement's Irish co-ordinator, James Stephens took the unusual step
of publishing a newspaper, *The Irish People*, carrying within
its pages constant threats of open and armed insurrection.[2]
Dublin Castle had its own network of active spies peppered
through the Fenian ranks, resulting in the arrest of the entire
editorial staff of *The Irish People*, at its city centre office, in
September, 1865. Stephens temporarily evaded arrest but in
November he was captured and lodged along with several
other leading figures in the Richmond Bridewell, on the South
Circular Road. Within days of his arrest he had master-
minded a daring escape throwing the administration of Dublin
Castle into a frenzy.[3] Arrangements were made at this time to
relocate the female prisoners in the gaol of Kilmainham to
other city centre prisons, while the ordinary male criminals in
Kilmainham were moved to Mountjoy Prison, on the North
Circular Road. Kilmainham Gaol was now given over by its
board of superintendents to the government for the safe custody
of all persons connected with treasonable practises, and the exchequer made available money to further strengthen security
within the prison.[4]

Following discussions with Governor Price, it was decided
that each cell located in the new wing and containing a political prisoner would be fitted with bolts, hasps, and padlocks
and covering the keyhole of the standard locks. Only two
master keys existed, one in the custody of the governor, who
kept it in his private quarters and the deputy governor retained the second.

Twelve check gates were erected along the prison corridors,

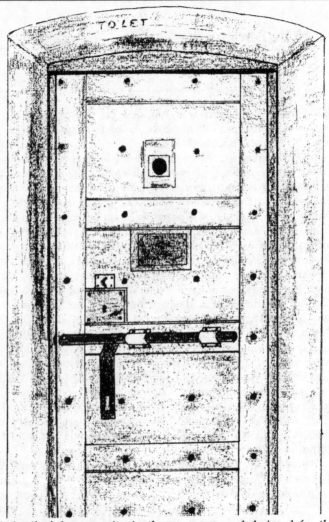

A detail of door security in the new compound designed for the security of the Fenian prisoners (1865-1867) complete with bolts, hasp, chubb lock, standard lock and padlock. Note the Judas or spy hole. (Drawing by Martin Crawford.)

and in addition one warder stood at each side of the large gates which divided the male from the female side of the prison. A round-the-clock military guard was placed inside and outside the prison walls; a constant military presence occupied the adjoining courthouse.[5] The prison was safe from attack without and escape from within.

Many prisoners were transferred from the Richmond Bridewell into Kilmainham in January of 1866 including John O'Leary, the editor of *The Irish People* and one of the leaders of the Fenian movement. Also transferred was Jeremiah O'Donovan Rossa, a devoted Nationalist and business manager of *The Irish People* newspaper.[6]

Christopher O'Keeffe and Charles Kickham received a sentence of fourteen years penal servitude, but Kickham was transferred from Kilmainham to the ageing model prison, Pentonville, and later to the gaols of Portland and Woking. He was finally released due to bad health in 1869 and thereafter he concentrated on writing.

By February of 1866 Kilmainham had over 200 prisoners charged with treasonable conspiracy, including Francis Nugent Cavanagh with an address at 37, Bayview Avenue, North Strand, Dublin, suspected of being a Fenian agent. He was released from Kilmainham on 24 August 1866 and sailed for America in late September.[7]

Denis Cashman was received into Governor Price's custody in March 1866. Under close questioning, alternating with periods of isolation in one of the punishment cells, he admitted that he was at one time a member of the Fenian conspiracy. Cashman served seven years in Kilmainham Gaol.[8]

The Fenian leadership was disunited abroad while in Ireland the membership rose to 50,000. During 1866 James Stephens travelled to America and against his better judgement was forced to order a rising for early 1867 while the date finally agreed upon was 5 March. There were men, but there were no arms. In Dublin and as far north as Louth and all over Munster, police barracks were attacked. As a result of the events of 5, 6, 7 March, over 600 arrests were made into Kilmainham.[9]

Each political prisoner sent to Kilmainham was confined to

his cell for twenty-three hours a day, under heavy military guard. For a short period they were allowed to read books selected by the governor, until it was discovered that the men were sending messages of support to each other in marking out words by underlining them with their fingernails. For one hour every day each political prisoner in Kilmainham exercised alone in one of the prison yards. Meanwhile, at 4.45 pm seven ounces of bread and half a pint of sweet milk for supper were placed in each political cell.

Every day at 5 pm the prison bell rang summoning them to stand outside the door of their cells for inspection. On the arrival of the governor, each called out his number and stepped back into his cell shutting the door behind him. This was then locked, tested and double locked, with bolts and hasps put firmly in place under the supervision of the governor, or in his absence, Thomas Flewett, newly appointed deputy governor. From October to April all prisoners had light supplied to their cells between the hours of five and seven in the evening. The light remained on all night in the cells of the political prisoners, who were checked every fifteen minutes by the night watchmen.

On admission to the gaol each prisoner was photographed by Flewett, for which the deputy governor was paid the sum of two shillings for every mug shot. Copies were sent to Dublin Castle as well as to other prisons and this made the detection of previous offenders a simple task. A man accused of stealing a mare was recognised through his photograph and when enquiries were made, he was found to be innocent and released from Kilmainham.

By 1868 most of the Kilmainham political prisoners had been removed to other prisons or released in exchange for information, while the large American contingent was ordered to sail home. Amongst these prisoners was John Clewn, originally from County Clare, Luke Collery from Cuffe Street, Dublin who had emigrated involuntarily after the Young Irelanders 1848 Rising, Thomas Meagher, Thomas Costello and Edmund Coyne, an USA army lieutenant.[10]

Governor Price died in 1873 leaving the prison crank pump as a legacy to Kilmainham. This was used to draw water from an

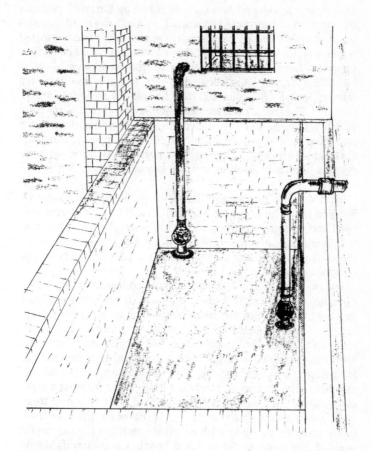

Kilmainham's punishment bath; over five feet deep, it was filled to capacity with cold water. It was used as a means of extracting information, without leaving marks on the body. The steam valves are situated in perforated form at the end of each pipe. When information was not forthcoming under cold water, the steam valve was turned on. Not used after the formation of the General Prison's Board in 1878. (Drawing by Martin Crawford.)

underground well and had been designed by him with patience during 1866. Constructed on a shaft principle the crank handles were independent of each other. A tell-tale rack indicated when a specified amount of labour had been completed. The prisoners working this were separated from each other in a box-like structure, but were allowed to rest, one at a time for a ten minute period which ensured that they all did an equal amount of work. The frame itself formed a series of compartments from which the main shaft extended through the machine. Each crank had at one end a pall which worked opposite a ratchet wheel, in turn passing through the partitioned framework, to prevent the men working it from communicating with each other.[11]

In 1874 the punishment cells, which previous to the rebuilding had stone floors, were boarded. The cells were frequently used and prisoners under punishment were given blankets and not sheets contrary to the 1826 Prisons Act (Amended) which directed that in addition to blankets one pair of sheets was to be allocated to each bed.

The erection of a new prison hospital concluded the rebuilding since parliament had made provision for the removal from prisons of the criminally insane to medically supervised institutions. The Kilmainham Gaol hospital accommodated the male and female sick prisoners in two large wards fitted out with water closets in each. Two smaller wards were set aside for patients with diseases which posed a risk of cross infection to others. Prevention was deemed essential as infections especially of the skin were easily transmitted, and effective treatment was limited and long term. Warders assigned to these prisoner patients, along with one male and one female medic, worked and lived in the isolated hospital accommodation to minimise the risk, not only to themselves but to the inmates as well.[12]

By 1872 the female prisoners were confined exclusively within the old west wing, where they lived in proximity to the ground floor laundry in which a ten hour working day, six days a week was operated. The number of female admissions rose sharply mainly due to the fact that the Four Courts Marshalsea was finally closed, and the number of women on charges of drunk and disorderly behaviour spiralled.[13] This over-crowding frequently resulted in the breakdown of prison discipline.

The supply of potatoes to Kilmainham Gaol during the early 1870s was again difficult to maintain owing to another crop failure. In consequence the medical members of the board of superintendents recommended the substitution of good bread three days a week, to be taken with vegetable soup. This was made up as follows:–

Add to one gallon of boiling water 8 oz. oatmeal.
Blend in a little cold water.
2 lbs. of turnips peeled or sliced.
4 ozs. onions cut small and as much pepper and
salt as will make it palatable.

Parsnips or carrots could be substituted for the turnips while the bread was ordered to be of wholemeal, and of equal parts flour and meal.

Supper was introduced in Kilmainham for all classifications of prisoners in 1873. This consisted of six ounces of bread and a half pint of one day old milk. Those prisoners who were Roman Catholic were bound to observe the season of Lent by receiving in place of milk two ounces of molasses for breakfast, and black tea at supper time, on each Wednesday and Friday during the lenten period.

Captain James McNeill Dyer, a retired naval officer, was appointed governor of Kilmainham in 1874, but died before he had completed one year in office and was replaced by Captain James Gray.

Prison reform was once more before parliament.

13. Parnell and the Invincibles

The establishment of the General Prisons Board of Ireland came into effect on 9 October 1877. Kilmainham and thirty-one other county gaols as well as ninety-five bridewells came under its jurisdiction.[1]

The establishment of the board did nothing to alter penal principles nor did it provide any improvement since the legislators of the time were concerned that the primary and essential object of a prison sentence was that it would be penal and deterrent. It leaned heavily on the theory and practice of reformatory methods such as Howard had introduced nearly a century before. Since the introduction of gas as a means of light the economic climate within the prison was of tantamount importance. The employment of prisoners aimed to achieve three objects. Firstly, to create a deterrent effect on the prisoner and on the criminal classes in general; secondly, to produce a reformatory effect on the prisoner, and thirdly to recoup as far as possible the cost of maintaining the prisoner and the prison.[2]

The position of inspectors general was eliminated resulting in each prison functioning as an autonomous body under the office of the lord lieutenant. In the prisons of Carlow, Cavan, Ennis and Lifford, untried prisoners *Only* were to be confined. Many of the older officers of these establishments were retired, bringing about an over-all saving within the service of £4,000.

By 1880 the general prisons board had the women prisoners in Kilmainham industriously engaged full-time in manufacturing prison clothing for the prison populations of Kilmainham and Mountjoy. Library books were formally available within the county prisons of Ireland and the choice and selection of reading matter was made by the prison chaplains. By and large the reading material lacked stimulus, being mainly of a spiritual nature.[3] Deprived of the freedom of conversation with his fellow inmate, the Kilmainham prisoner was cloistered in a monastic atmosphere.

No evidence survives of any special interest taken in any prisoner in Kilmainham by schoolmaster wardens. The chaplain's influence was non-existent, since he had to reach every single prisoner in turn during his weekly visits, in order to comply with the standing orders of his brief since the establishment of the Prisons Board. This emerged as a formality rather than a system of support to the Kilmainham inmate.

Prisoners in Kilmainham now rose at 6.30 am, when the sound of the prison bell instructed them to vacate their beds, wash, and cleanse their cells. At 6.45 am unlock was conducted under the supervision of the deputy governor, and early morning exercise was in progress at 7 am clearing all prisoners from the cell area. Methodical searches were then made in the interests of prison security. The prisoners breakfasted at 8.30 am and were locked up until 9.30 am while the warders broke fast together. Work commenced in all areas of the prison at 9.30 am until dinner was served at one o'clock.[4] Dinner was taken in the central hall on trestle type tables, in the presence of a heavy military guard. The men served themselves and cleared up after the meal. A half-hour of school immediately followed. The female prisoners ate in their cells.[5]

The afternoon work schedule was in progress at 2 pm sharp for those prisoners under sentence of hard labour. Others were detailed for special cleaning or decorative duties within the prison on the instructions of the governor. The last meal of the day in Kilmainham was now shared by the men once more in the compound followed by a short religious talk by the visiting chaplain, each pastor collecting his own congregation in a corner of the hall. Lock-up for the night commenced at 6 pm. Lights were now allowed to remain on in the cells until 7.45 pm when each prisoner was left with his own thoughts, and more than his share of loneliness.

On Sundays the day did not commence until 7.15 am when, after breakfast, a choice was given to attend religious services or remain locked up for the day.[6] Most of the male prisoners opted for attendance in church, since bodily as well as spiritual exchange could take place there, and it was by far the brightest part of the prison, with its decorative altar and large windows. It was warm when the sun shone through the bars on the outside. The present altar in the Catholic Church of Kilmainham Gaol was built by a prisoner, James Lalor, and the following inscription on a piece of wood incorporated in the altar reads:

> Pray for the person who made and put up this altar with the assistance of a boy......I James Lalor, serving seven years penal servitude.[7]

It bears the date August, 1882.[8]

With the formation of the General Prisons Board the punishment cells in Kilmainham ceased to operate, as prisoners under punishment for breach of prison discipline were confined to their own cells on a diet of bread and water for a maximum of three days. Then they would be returned to a normal diet for another three days, and revert back to the punishment diet until the period of punishment specified by the governor had been completed.

Prisoners in Kilmainham under medical supervision had their diet supplemented by bacon, beef tea, biscuits, butter, cake, cocoa, cornflour, eggs, as well as a choice of fruit and greens.[9]

Charles Stewart Parnell was at the height of his political power at this time. Elected as a Member of Parliament, one of a group agitating for Home Rule, and placed in the constituency of Meath in 1875, the Avondale, Co. Wicklow born Parnell possessed a mastery of parliamentary procedure not previously encountered in Westminster.[10]

By 1879 Michael Davitt, born in the same year as Parnell, 1846, founded the Irish Land League. The basic policy of the Land League was to acquire the land of Ireland for the people of Ireland, and Parnell was invited by Davitt to become the Society's first president. Parnell accepted and because of Land League agitation was arrested and lodged as a guest of the ageing Victoria in Kilmainham Gaol, on 13 October 1881, in spite of his high political profile. The Land League was outlawed in 1882.

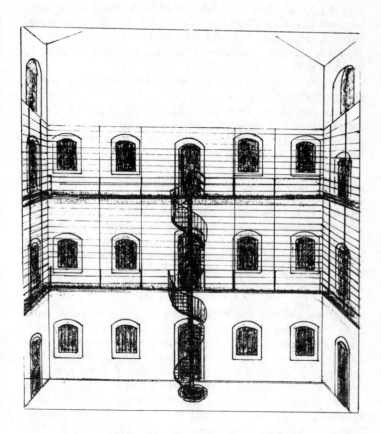

Detail of spiral staircase in the new (1864) east wing. ONLY prisoners used this, the idea being that as long as a man was going round and round at a fast pace he could not get into mischief. Also he was visible at all times of ascent and descent. (Drawing by Martin Crawford.)

During his incarceration in Kilmainham, Parnell gave the question of the land a great deal of thought.[11] He believed that the defeat of landlordism should be replaced by a system of small tenant holdings. In this respect he had given parliament an assurance that the introduction of an Arrears Bill would facilitate the working of the Land Act, which came into effect in 1881.

The incarceration of such an important figure caused concern within Dublin Castle, as well as to the governor of Kilmainham, as they feared rumours of bad treatment would run rife throughout the country, and perhaps result in the storming of the prison. To ensure that any such rumour was without foundation, a room was set aside for Parnell's exclusive use within the central corridors of Kilmainham, between the new east wing and the old west wing. This had certainly been used as a visitors' room for some years, and was opposite the condemned cell.[12] Parnell's room remained unlocked for most of the time and he had access to anyone he wanted to see from inside or outside of the prison, at any time of the day or night. Many of the other Land League prisoners in Kilmainham at the same time believed that Parnell had his own set of keys and could come and go as he liked, although there is no evidence that he had.

Following Parnell into Kilmainham in quick succession, came John Dillon and William O'Brien. During their time in gaol the 'Kilmainham Treaty' was signed, when British Premier Gladstone came to terms with Parnell. This resulted in the cessation of agitation by the Land League and the unconditional release of Dillon, Michael Davitt and Parnell. The rent arrears negotiations with the government were opened immediately, with the recurring fear of rebellion always present. These negotiations resulted in the immediate drafting of an Arrears Bill based on measures which had been proposed by Parnell and Dillon, and it was introduced without delay.[13]

As a result William Edward Forster, chief secretary to the lord lieutenant in Ireland resigned in protest and was replaced by Lord Frederick Charles Cavendish.[14] On the evening of 6 May 1882, four days after Parnell's release, the newly appointed Cavendish was strolling through the Phoenix Park, with T.H. Burke, his under-secretary. The men had only just met the previous day and they were assassinated by five members of the Invincibles, a secret society formed in Dublin in 1881. The Invincibles stood outside the Fenian body and were composed of a breakaway element of men drawn from its ranks. Their oath of allegiance pledged them to obey all orders without question under penalty of death.

Within days, six members of the Invincibles were captured and held in Kilmainham. The early arrests came mostly through the age old informer network. Five of the Invincibles were hanged behind the high prison walls of Kilmainham for the murders of Burke and Cavendish. They were Joseph Brady, a stonecutter employed by Dublin Corporation executed on 14 May 1883; Daniel Curley, who ran a small tobacconist's shop with his wife, executed on 18 May; Michael Fagan, a blacksmith (22), Thomas Caffrey (25) who worked on Dublin Quays, and Timothy Kelly, a nineteen year old coachbuilder, who lived in the vicinity of Manor Street, executed on 9 June.[15]

In accordance with procedure the governor supervised the erection of the scaffolding at the last minute. All details had been kept secret and the wood for the erection of the gallows had only arrived into the prison late on the night previous to the first execution. The equipment had been ordered by written application from Mountjoy where all accessories for the purpose of execution were kept in accordance with general prisons board rules, and supplied when required to the requesting prison. These included the rope, the pinioning apparatus (although Marwood the executioner who travelled from London to perform these executions had designed his own restraint strap 'to prevent the culprit from struggling'). Also part of the equipment was the standard white cap, placed over the condemned man's face before the rope was secured around his neck to prevent the official party in attendance from seeing the facial contortions of the victim in his death throes.

There was also the bag, capable of containing the same weight of sand as the condemned prisoner. This was designed with a very thick neck, well padded from the outside, and by regulation had a soft canvas padding to prevent damage to the hangman's rope! The rope itself was tested before each execution 'by a competent officer' for fear of defect.[16]

On the night before the execution of Timothy Kelly, the gas-lit corridors of Kilmainham Gaol resounded with the sound of Kelly's mature voice. He was an avid enthusiast of amateur musicals, and along with Brady sang in the choir in Church Street. The prison was deathly still as Kelly sang away his last hours in clear musical tones. Without any tremor whatsoever in his voice, he sang the patriot song 'The Memory of the Past'. His strong voice echoed throughout the gaol.

Behind the closed doors of night time in Kilmainham on that June night in 1883 even the most hardened of men shared Timothy Kelly's last hours.

After each execution a coroner's inquest was held and the verdict posted publicly outside the gate of the prison. Immediately upon pronouncement of death by the prison doctor, a black flag was hoisted high from one of the chimneys of Kilmainham. In each case a huge crowd gathered outside.

The coroner's verdict in the case of Kelly, Brady, Fagan, and Curley was recorded as 'Death by rupture of the spinal cord in the neck from hanging' while the verdict on Caffrey was 'Death by Asphyxiation' in that the rope was not effective in rupturing the spinal cord at the neck.

The next day, the deed done, life in Kilmainham returned to normal, the sounds of the stonebreakers at work in the yard to the front of the prison could be heard by the passers-by. Inside the bell rang in summons to meals, work and prayers, accompanied as always by the jangling sound of keys.

Between 1883 and 1896 Kilmainham Gaol had a change of governor four times. In turn the new appointees were Captain St. George Grey, Captain Rudolph Gildea, who had charge of Charles S. Parnell, Mr. J. Leslie Beard and A.D. Manus.

14. Freedom

With the opening years of the twentieth century, the glorious period of elegance in Dublin of the late eighteenth and early nineteenth century had faded. Dublin was now a jaded entity, and the tensions of rebellion had taken its toll . Houses that once were grand and proud now functioned as over-crowded tenement hovels. Kilmainham Gaol was allowed to deteriorate further, and closed for the reception of prisoners in February of 1910 giving way to the expanding Mountjoy Prison.[1]

In 1912 Prime Minister Asquith introduced the Third Home Rule Bill for Ireland. The Ulster Volunteers led by Edward Carson organised themselves determined to defeat it.[2]

In 1913 William Martin Murphy and other employers formed a Federation to combat the swelling Irish Transport and General Workers Union, founded by James Connolly and James Larkin.[3] In order to force their employees to leave the union they were locked out of their jobs. Consequently 25,000 people were unemployed for six months until they could no longer hold out and returned to work. Street clashes occurred frequently and as a result James Connolly founded the Irish Citizen Army –an armed body born with the spirit of self defence. He was supported by the Countess Markievicz.

Eoin MacNeill established the Irish Volunteers in 1914 and in August 1914 England declared war on Germany. John Redmond, leader of the Irish Party at Westminster urged the Irish Volunteers to join the British army.

Kilmainham Gaol was taken over by the Military to accommodate the extra recruitment of troops and remained in military control until after the 1916 Irish Rebellion.

A large number of people rejected Redmond's advice and joined the Irish Republican Brotherhood. Behind the Irish Republican Brotherhood was Pádraig Pearse, a schoolteacher who had founded his own college, St. Endas, Rathfarnham, intent on teaching the principles of education through the medium of Irish. Pádraig Pearse, Thomas Clarke, a dedicated Republican, Thomas MacDonagh, Pádraig's close friend, Eamonn Ceannt, a long time member of the IRB, joined forces with James Connolly, Seán MacDermott, Joseph Mary Plunkett and Seán Heuston to form the Military Council in preparation and readiness to plan for rebellion.[4] All believed in taking advantage of England's war with Germany.

Eoin MacNeill was opposed to the idea of a rebellion that was certain to be defeated, but in spite of this Pádraig Pearse led a column of men which included his younger brother, Willie (from whom he was inseparable), James Connolly and Thomas Clarke from Liberty Hall, to occupy the General Post Office on Easter Monday, 1916. At 12.15 pm on that day Pádraig Pearse flanked by the faithful Clarke, read the Proclamation of the Provisional Government of Ireland, from the steps of the post office. For six days fierce fighting ensued as the city centre went up in flames.

Pearse was finally forced to order a surrender to prevent the further loss of life in Dublin, and to save the lives of followers now surrounded and hopelessly out-numbered by the swelling British reinforcements. Ninety-seven of the leaders were sentenced to death by English court-martials which were later commuted to penal servitude.

Kilmainham Gaol was quickly brought back into action again as a high security prison, and large numbers of prisoners were lodged there, including eighty-five of the Cumann na mBan Movement, the Women Auxiliary Force.

The number of male prisoners confined in Kilmainham following court-martials at Arbour Hill and Richmond Detention Barracks included five of the signatories of the Proclamation. In all, fourteen of the leaders of the Easter Rising faced the firing squad in Kilmainham Gaol. Roger Casement was hanged in London, and Thomas Kent was shot in Cork. Eamonn de Valera, who had occupied Bolands Mills and Westland Row Railway Station at the head of 130 men had his death sentence commuted. Countess Markievicz also received sentence of death, but this too was commuted since the authorities were fearful that the execution of a woman would bring about an emotional reaction from the people of Dublin.

Kilmainham Gaol was once again bulging with patriots. Conditions within the gaol were atrocious since most of the original structure of the prison had been in disuse for six years. There was no light in any of the cells in the old west wing, where the leaders were dumped in darkness awaiting the inevitable death sentence and execution by firing squad.

There was no special diet, no favourable conditions, no privileges accorded to the condemned men. The men were confident, no matter what the outcome, that they had furthered the cause of Irish freedom. There was not much time to set personal affairs in order. The letter of the law had to be carried out with military precision, and at the appointed time.

During Pádraig Pearse's last hours in Kilmainham it is reported that he wrote his poem 'The Wayfarer', and he responded to the sentence of the court martial passed upon him acknowledging that when he was a boy of ten he dreamed that one day he would die for Ireland. His statement concludes: 'You cannot extinguish the Irish passion for freedom. If our deed has not been sufficient to win freedom, then our children will win it by a better deed.' Pearse was attended by Father Aloysius from the Capuchin Friary, Church Street, who together with Father Augustine and Father Sebastian provided spiritual and moral support for the men during those last lonely hours in Kilmainham Gaol.[5]

Late on the night of 2 May, hours before his execution, Pearse wrote a letter of goodbye to his mother, including a note to this young brother Willie, also captured and lodged in Kilmainham, unknown to Pearse.[6]

At midnight as Pearse was penning his last lines of poetry, his great friend Thomas MacDonagh was writing from his cell at Kilmainham – 'I'm ready to die at dawn. My country will reward my deed richly'. His sister, a nun at Basin Lane convent came to see her brother for the last time, accompanied by Father Aloysius.

Tom Clarke was executed with Pádraig Pearse and Thomas MacDonagh on 3 May. Tom Clarke left a message to the Irish people, which his family had published as a Memoriam Card in 1917. This reads:

> I and my fellow signatories believe we have struck
> the first successful blow for freedom. The next blow we
> have no doubt Ireland will strike will win through. In
> this belief we die happy.

Clarke spent an hour with his wife in his cell before execution. A soldier was present during the interview holding a candle in a jam jar. Clarke expressed the relief that he was to be executed fearing only that he would have to serve yet another prison sentence. He had spent a total of 18 years in British prisons for his allegiance to the Republican Movement.

As Pádraig Pearse stood facing the firing squad, his brother Willie was being brought handcuffed and under military escort to the place of execution for a last visit. As the soldiers were bringing him into the yard adjacent to the stonebreaker's yard, the site chosen for execution, a volley of shots was heard, preventing the brothers from bidding each other goodbye.

At 6 pm on the evening of 3 May while the prison population of Kilmainham was dismayed by the executions of Pádraig Pearse, Thomas Clarke and Thomas MacDonagh, a young girl named Grace Gifford, the childhood sweetheart of Joseph Plunkett entered Kilmainham Gaol. For two hours she was left alone to walk about in one of the prison yards, while her fiance was transferred from Richmond Barracks to Kilmainham, in readiness for their wedding which took place hours before his execution in the Catholic chapel of the prison. The young couple had originally planned to marry on Easter Sunday, but the rising had postponed the event, and Grace promised Joseph that if he was captured she would marry him in prison. She was here now to honour that promise and to show her love for her patriot sweetheart.

At exactly 8 pm Grace was escorted to the Catholic chapel, and as she entered from the door at the rear, her fiance was led in through a door near the altar by a party of soldiers with fixed bayonets.

The ceremony was performed in candlelight, by Father Eugene McCarthy, because of a gas failure earlier in the day.[7]

Immediately afterwards the young couple were separated, Joseph to return to his cell, and Grace to lodgings in nearby Thomas Street, found for her by the priest. Several hours later she was called again to the gaol, and the bride and groom were allowed to spend ten minutes together in a cell, before being parted finally.

At dawn on 4 May 1916 Joseph faced the firing squad along with young Willie Pearse, Edward Daly and Michael O'Hanrahan.[8]

The people of Dublin were in time to become sickened by the executions, while within Kilmainham Gaol more sacrifices were being prepared with the lives of Major John MacBride, Seán Heuston, Michael Mallin and Eamonn Ceannt. They were executed on 8 May.

MacBride, estranged husband of Maud Gonne, was seen in Parnell Square, Dublin, on Easter Sunday while on Monday he chose to fight because in his own words 'he detested British rule so much'.[9]

Heuston received only a few hours notice of sentence of death and sent for his family to share his last moments. His brother, a clerical student in the Dominican Priory, Tallaght, came immediately in response to the call. Seán, from his Kilmainham cell wrote to his sister, Mary, a Dominican nun in Galway. She would receive her brother's last words only after the volley of shots resounded once more through the prison, taking four more Irish lives.

Seán Mac Diarmada was the last of the leaders imprisoned in Kilmainham to face the firing squad. He was visited by his girlfriend Mary Ryan and her sister, Phyllis, in his small Kilmainham cell.[10] Seán placed an arm around each of the girls and talked of happy times, until Father McCarthy, came to commence that long procession and last journey.[11]

James Connolly, the last man to be executed in Kilmainham, was never a prisoner there. Immediately after the surrender, Connolly, because of a bad leg wound, was taken to a hospital wing, functioning somewhere in the bowels of Dublin Castle. From his hospital bed he was court-martialled and sentenced to die in Kilmainham. His last journey through Dublin was in a Red Cross ambulance, which entered the gaol though the gate furthest from the courthouse.

In all, fourteen executions took place in Kilmainham in the weeks following Easter 1916 on dates between 3 May and 12 May. The site chosen for the executions, all of which took place at dawn, was the stonebreaker's yard where many a prisoner had his spirit broken over the years. The stonebreaker's yard is the only site in the prison that cannot be overlooked from the prison building. It is separated by a high wall and was chosen so that nobody from a prison cell would bear witness to the fourteen Irish lives offered up in sacrifice after Easter Week, 1916.[12]

By 1920 Kilmainham Gaol was once more functioning as a prison, with members of the Irish Republican Army occupying the new compound, as well as the old west wing. The central corridors of the prison, dividing the two, were filled with vigilant British military guards.

Occupying three cells within the old west wing, on 14 February 1921 among other Republicans, were Ernie O'Malley, Simon Donnolly and Frank Teeling, who with the help of a friendly warder effected a daring escape to freedom through one of the gates of Kilmainham. O'Malley was using the name Stewart, while Teeling was under sentence of death and both would certainly have been hanged. The escape was successful only on a second attempt. On the first occasion, Patrick Moran, a Republican prisoner awaiting trial for a crime he played no part in had joined O'Malley, Teeling and Donnolly, but when they got to the gate, the bolt cutters necessary to forge a thrush through the gate bolts proved ineffective. The men had to abandon their attempt and try again, but this time Patrick Moran in fear for the safety of his witnesses refused to go.[13] Patrick Moran was hanged in Mountjoy Gaol following a trial which brought back a verdict of guilty.

When civil war broke out in 1922 Kilmainham Gaol was taken over by the Free State Government. Only women prisoners were confined there. By and large conditions were good, and the prisoners were treated well. The wardresses who guarded them came from Mountjoy Prison. The women had

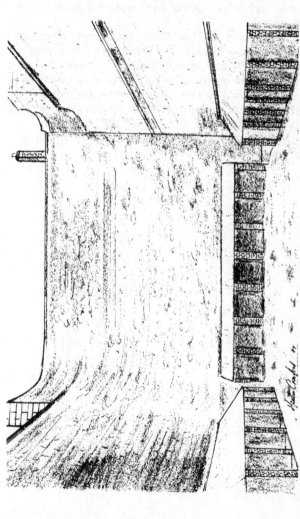

Stonebreaker's Yard, Kilmainham Gaol. The huts were constructed especially for the prisoner who was too old, too weak, too sick or too infirmed to be able to take his place with the able bodied crews at work in the centre of the yard. (Drawing by Martin Crawford from an original photograph in the Kilmainham Gaol Archives.) It was the site chosen for the 14 executions of the leaders of the Easter rebellion of 1916.

freedom in so far as their cell doors were left open all day, and they could visit each other. One of these women prisoners was Grace Plunkett.[14]

The first executions of the Civil War took place in Kilmainham on 17 November, 1922. These were James Fisher, Peter Cassidy, John F. Gaffney and Richard Twohig.[15]

The last political prisoner held in Kilmainham was Eamonn de Valera, in 1923, and finally Kilmainham Gaol closed its doors in 1924. A formal order of closure was passed through Dáil Éireann in 1929.

The Dismal House of Little Ease would imprison Irishmen and Irishwomen no more.

Chapter Notes

Chapter One
1. *Documents Relating to Ireland*, J.S. Gilbert, Dollard Press, Dublin, 1894.
2. *Dublin and Its Topography*, S.A. Ossory Fitzpatrick, Methuen Books London, 1907.
3. *Knights of St. John of Jerusalem*, J.S. Gilbert, Dollard Press, Dublin, 1892.
4. From *The Journal of the Royal Society of Antiquitaries*, RSAI, Fitzwilliam Square, Dublin. Volume 32.
5. *The Neighbourhood of Dublin*, Weston St. John Joyce, Gill, Dublin, 1912.
6. *Dublin*, Peter Somerville Large, Hamish Hamilton, London, 1970.
7. *The Ormonde Papers*, contained in the volume relating to *Public Works, 17th Century*, Irish State Paper Office, Dublin.
8. *Chronicles of Ireland*, John Holinshed, Constable, London, 1898.
9. *Dublin*, Peter Somerville Large, Hamish Hamilton, London, 1970.
10. *The Ormonde Papers*, Dublin under Public Works, Ref OP –Irish State Paper Office.
11. *Irish Life in the 17th Century*, Edward MacLysaght, Irish Academic Press, Dublin, 1979.

Chapter Two
1. *A Consideration of Ireland in the 18th Century*, Locker Lampson, Constable, London, 1907.
2. *State of the Prisons*, John Howard, Warrington Press, England, 1784.
3. *Ordnance Survey Name Book*, Office of the Ordnance Survey, Dublin.
4. *The Dublin Historical Record*, Old Dublin Society, Volume XXXV.
5. *The Fabrication of Virtue*, Robin Evans, Cambridge University Press, 1982.
6. Prisoner Petition, Letter Sir F. Englesfield, as reproduced in *The Fabrication of Virtue*, Robin Evans, Cambridge University Press, 1982.
7. *Life of John Howard*, compiled by Walter Venning, from Howard's personal documents, Allardice Press, Edinburgh, 1825.
8. *The State of the Prisons in Ireland and England*, by John Howard, Warrington, England, 1777.
9. *The Fabrication of Virtue*, Robin Evans, Cambridge University Press, 1982.
10. *Parliamentary Papers for the year 1778*, Reference HMSO, National Library of Ireland.

11.   *The Dublin Historical Record*, Old Dublin Society (on file in the Gilbert Memorial Library, Pearse Street), Volume XXXVII.

Chapter Three

1.   *The Course of Irish History*, edited by T.W. Moody and F.X. Martin, Mercier Press, Cork & Dublin, in conjunction with RTE, second edition 1984

2.   *Dublin*, Peter Somerville Large, Hamish Hamilton, London, 1970.

3.   *The Fabrication of Virtue*, Robin Evans, Cambridge University Press, 1982.

4.   *Parliamentary Papers for the year 1782*, ref HMSO, National Library of Ireland, Kildare Street.

5.   *ACTS* 26. George III. Cap 74.

6.   *Documents relating to Kilmainham Gaol*, on file in the Irish Architectural Archives, Merrion Square, Dublin.

7.   *Documents relating to Dublin's Newgate Prison*, as found in Official Papers, 1783, Irish State Paper Office, Dublin Castle.

8.   *Irish Parliamentary Papers for the year 1783*, Ref HMSO, National Library of Ireland, Kildare Street.

9.   *The Life of John Howard*, compiled by Walter Venning, from Howard's personal documents, Allardice Press, Edinburgh, 1825.

10.   *Official Papers, Ref OP*, Irish State Paper Office, Dublin Castle.

11.   Act 26th of George III. Cap 74.

12.   *Circular (undated) issued by the Court of Kings Bench*, to the residents of Kilmainham, which can be found on file in the Official Papers correspondence, Ref OP 1786, Irish State Paper Office, Dublin Castle.

13.   *Documents (copy)* relating to 1798 on file in Kilmainham Gaol Archives, from Doctor R.R. Madden's *United Irishmen*, United Irishman newspaper, 1846.

14.   *Faulkner's Dublin Journal*, printed by J.Brooks, Dublin, 1804.

Chapter Four

1.   *The History of Prisons*, John Howard, Warrington, England, 1779.

2.   John Traile's Plan of Kilmainham Gaol (circa 1788) – See illustration on Page 27. Original map now in possession of the Office of Public Works, Architectural Division, Stephen's Green. Copy in Gaol Archives.

3.   *The Memories of Jemmy Hope*, an autobiography of a working-class United Irishman, first published in the *United Irishman*, now on microfilm National Library of Ireland, Kildare Street, by Doctor R.R.Madden.

4.   *The Making of Modern Ireland*, J.C. Beckett, Faber and Faber, London, 1966.

5.   *The Fabrication of Virtue*, Robin Evans, Cambridge University Press, 1982.

6. John Traile's Plan of Kilmainham Gaol 1796 now on file Gaol Archives.

7. *Prisons*, M. Hamblin Smith, Bodley Head Press, 1934.

8. The petition of Robert Ware to Lord Lieutenant found in the Official Papers, Irish State Paper Office – Ref: 87/1A.

9. *The Journal of the Irish House of Commons*, for the year 1797, Appendix 203, National Library of Ireland.

10. *The Life and Times of Mary Ann McCracken*, Mary   McNeill, Figgis, Dublin, 1960.

11. Petition of Robert Ware, found amongst the Official Papers, Irish State Paper Office – a copy of which is now in Kilmainham Gaol Archives.

12. The petition of Henry Haslett, dated 27 June 1797, discovered in correspondence entitled 'Prisoners Petitions and Correspondence', Irish State Paper Office, copy of which is now in the Kilmainham Gaol Archives.

13. *The Life and Times of Robert Emmet*, Dr. R.R. Madden, J.J. Duffy, Dublin, 1847.

14. *Kilmainham* – the Booklet, Trustees of Kilmainham Gaol, 1961.

15. The petition of Susannah Richardson, Official Papers correspondence, Irish State Paper Office – Ref: OP/87 1B.

16. *John Philpott Curran, His Life and Times*, Leslie Hale, Cape, 1958.

Chapter Five

1. *A Consideration of Ireland in the 18th Century*,   Locker Lampson, Constable, London, 1907.

2. Cornwallis Correspondence relating to the Rebellion and the aftermath of 1798, Official Papers, 1800, Irish State Paper Office.

3. There are at least 150 documented prisoners' petitions in support of the claims made within this book in relation to the cruelty of Edward Trevor. The source used were SIXTEEN cartons of correspondence in the Irish State Paper Office entitled 'Prisoners petitions and correspondence'. A copy of each of these has now been lodged in the Kilmainham Gaol Archives.

4. Amongst these were the petitions of Bernard Coile, James Tandy (son of Napper Tandy), Philip Long, David Fitzgerald. Anne Devlin in her *Prison Journal*, edited by John Finegan (Mercier Press 1968) demonstrates ample proof of Trevor's bestial nature.

5. The petition of James Power, Prisoners' Petitions and Correspondence, 60/154, Irish State Paper Office, Carton No. 3.

6. Prisoners' Petitions and Correspondence, 60/154, Irish State Paper Office.

7. Petition of Thomas O'Flanagan, August 1800, Prisoners' Petitions and Correspondence, 536, Irish State Paper Office.

8. The petition of Henry Morres, Prisoners' Petitions and Correspondence,

3938, Irish State Paper Office.

9. During research for this book over 300 letters in Edward Trevor's hand have been retrieved in copy form from the Irish State Paper Office, containing instructions and orders for the movement and treatment of prisoners. Copies now form part of the Kilmainham Gaol Archives.

10. The memorial of Bernard Coile, August 1805 found in documents relating to the Emmet Rebellion in Irish State Paper Office. Copy now in Kilmainham Gaol Archives.

11. Tandy's prison statement giving details of his Kilmainham experience was published by himself after his release from the prison in 1804. This can be found in a collection of pamphlets for the year 1805 in the National Library of Ireland.

12. The petition of Edward Newenham, from Kilmainham Gaol, dated 23 October 1800, copied from source at Irish State Paper Office and now in Kilmainham Gaol Archives.

13. The Letter of Winifred Doolan to Lord Lieutenant, Prisoners' Petitions and Correspondence, 353, Irish State Paper Office.

14. A note in handwriting of Dublin Castle official at the end of Newenham's petition, now in Kilmainham Gaol Archives.

15. Official Papers, OP 81/ Irish State Paper Office.

Chapter Six

1. *The Pursuit of Robert Emmet*, Helen Landreth, Richview Press, Dublin, 1949.

2. *The Life and Times of Robert Emmet*, Dr. R.R. Madden, J.J. Duffy, Dublin, 1847.

3. *The Voice of Sarah Curran*, her unpublished letters and full story of her life, Major-General H.G.MacMullen, CB, CBE, MC, privately printed and distributed by Greene's Library, Clare Street, Dublin.

4. The house is still there today, situated near the Garda Station, Rathfarnham.

5. Brother Luke Cullen, from conversations with Anne Devlin and subsequently published as *The Prison Journal of Anne Devlin* edited by John Finegan, Mercier Press, Cork, 1968, originals of which are in the National Library, Kildare Street.

6. One of Emmet's right hand men and in his complete trust. Formerly from Rathcoffey, Co. Kildare, Quigley betrayed many of the leaders of 1803 after Emmet's execution and became a pawn of Doctor Edward Trevor in Kilmainham Gaol. Later he opened a public house in Echlin Street, Dublin, on the fringe of Thomas Street, from funds provided from a secret service fund at Dublin Castle.

7. Philip Long, formerly a prisoner in Kilmainham Gaol following the 1798 rebellion, and again following Emmet's 1803 rising. His sister

Margaret Fitzgerald lived at 4, Crow Street, Dublin. Long was later banished to America.

8.   *Ireland in '98* – based on the published and unpublished manuscripts of Dr. R.R. Madden, Sonnenschein Press, 1842.

9.   Documents relating to Emmet's Rebellion, Irish State Paper Office, Ref 620/11/135.

10. Emmet's mother was Eileen Mason from near Killarney, Co. Kerry.

11. Documents relating to the questioning of the Devlin family in Dublin Castle, August 1803, Ref 620/11/138/8, Irish State Paper Office. Copies are now in the Kilmainham Gaol Archives.

12. *The Pursuit of Robert Emmet*, Helen Landreth, Richview Press, Dublin, 1949.

13. *The Prison Journal of Anne Devlin*, edited by John Finegan, from the Luke Cullen Manuscripts, Mercier Press, 1968.

14. The Kilmainham Gaol Register, August 1803, preserved in the Public Records Office, Dublin.

15. *The Pursuit of Robert Emmet*, Helen Landreth, Richview Press, Dublin, 1949.

16. *The Prison Journal of Anne Devlin*, edited by John Finegan, from the Luke Cullen Manuscripts, Mercier Press, 1968.

17. See illustration 1796 plan of Kilmainham Gaol on Page 27.

18. *Footprints of Emmet*, John Joseph Reynolds, Gill, Dublin, 1903, to mark the Emmet Centenary.

Chapter Seven

1.   *The Pursuit of Robert Emmet*, Helen Landreth, Richview Press, Dublin, 1949.

2.   The Kilmainham Gaol Register, 1803, preserved in the Public Records Office, Dublin.

3.   *Botany Bay*, Con Costello, Mercier Press, Cork & Dublin,1987.

4.   Official Papers Irish State Paper Office Ref: 267/6, copy of which is now in the Kilmainham Gaol Archives.

5.   *Botany Bay*, Con Costello, Mercier Press, Cork & Dublin,1987.

6.   Prisoners Petitions, Irish State Paper Office Ref Prisoners Petitions and Correspondence 1258 Dublin Castle, a copy is now in the Kilmainham Gaol Archives.

7.   Prisoners Petitions, Irish State Paper Office Ref Prisoners Petitions and Correspondence 1260 in Doctor Trevor's handwriting, dated 22 September , 1810, a copy of which is now in the Kilmainham Gaol Archives.

8.   Official Papers, Irish State Paper Office Ref: OP/298/9.

9.   The transfer is recorded in a letter from P.Callan, Secretary, House of Industry, an institution founded on the instructions of Parliament for the reform of the criminal character by penal labour. Situated in James

Street, the correspondence was addressed to the Honourable Robert Peel, Chief Secretary, Dublin Castle, dated 14 May 1814, Irish State Paper Office, Ref 36/4058. Copy now in Kilmainham Gaol Archives.

10. Prisoners Petitions, Ref Prisoners Petitions and Correspondence 1270, Irish State Paper Office, a copy is now in the Kilmainham Gaol Archives.

11. The visiting inspector was Henry Campbell, who lived in Prussia Street, Dublin.

12. Prisoners Petitions, Irish State Paper Office Ref Prisoners Petitions and Correspondence 4073, copy now in the Kilmainham Gaol Archives.

13. The circumstances relating to this can be borne out in a batch of correspondence attached to Hope's original petition, Prisoners Petitions and Correspondence Ref 1351 Irish State Paper Office. Copy of these now in the Kilmainham Gaol Archives.

14. Ref: Official papers for the year 1817, Irish State Paper Office, a copy now in the Kilmainham Gaol Archives.

Chapter Eight

1. Prisoners Petitions, Irish State Paper Office, Ref Prisoners Petitions and Correspondence Carton 12, a copy now in the Kilmainham Gaol Archives.

2. Note authorising release attached to above petition in the handwriting of Dublin Castle official, copies of both now lodged in the Kilmainham Gaol Archives.

3. Report from Board of Superintendents to the grand jury of the County of Dublin, dated March 1817 from official papers of that year, Irish State Paper Office, copies of both in the Kilmainham Gaol Archives.

4. Report of sub-committee sent into Kilmainham Gaol to enquire as to the present state of the prison, Registered Papers 1819 Ref RP 1819/P106 signed by Edward Groves, chairman of the gaol sub-committee and a member of the Dublin grand jury. A copy now in Kilmainham Gaol Archives.

5. *The Dublin Historical Record*, Old Dublin Society. All volume bound copies preserved in the Gilbert Memorial Library, Pearse Street.

6. Kilmainham Gaol Register, preserved in the Public Records Office, Dublin (1817).

7. The examination of George Dunn by Edward Trevor, Registered Papers, 1819, a copy is now in Kilmainham Gaol Archives.

8. This statement is on page four of above. Copy now in Kilmainham Gaol Archives.

9. Registered Papers 1819, P 106, Irish State Paper Office.

10. The report of the Inspectors General of Prisons, National Library of Ireland, Kildare Street, from Parliamentary Papers for the year 1819.

11. Parliamentary Papers 1796 giving report of progress of plans for the new Kilmainham Gaol, preserved in the National Library of Ireland, Kildare

Street, Dublin.

12. Report of Inspectors General of Prisons, (1820) in the National Library of Ireland, Kildare Street, Dublin. A copy now in Kilmainham Gaol Archives.

Chapter Nine

1. *Dublin*, Peter Somerville Large, Hamish Hamilton, London, 1970.
2. *Life of Mother Mary Aikenhead*, 'Irish Messenger Series', the Irish Messenger, 5 Denmark Street, Dublin, 1946.
3. *Life of Mother Mary Aikenhead*, 'Irish Messenger Series', the Irish Messenger, 5 Denmark Street, Dublin, 1946.
4. The Kilmainham Gaol Register, March, 1821, preserved in the Public Records Office, Dublin.
5. Archives, Sisters of Charity, Milltown, Dublin 6.
6. Notice of Sentence, Kilmainham Gaol Register, May 1821, preserved in Public Records Office, Dublin.
7. Statement of Fr. Thomas Luby, who attended the execution. Information provided by Mr. Mark Hyland, former Chairman, Kilmainham Gaol Board of Trustees.
8. Conversation with Sister Catherine, Irish Sisters of Charity, Crumlin.
9. Acts 1 & 2 George IV. Cap. 33.
10. Registered Papers 1823, Ref D 7742, Irish State Paper Office. A copy now in Kilmainham Gaol Archives.
11 Registered Papers 1823, Ref P. 172, Irish State Paper Office.
12. Registered Papers 1822, Ref P 1159, Irish State Paper Office.
13. Report, Inspectors General of Prisons, 1823, a copy of which is in the Irish State Paper Office.
14. Report, Inspectors General of Prisons, 1824, National Library of Ireland.
15. The Report of the Society for the Improvement of Prison Discipline, Signed by Robert White and Edward Groves, and dated 31 March 1824, Irish State Paper Office – a copy now in Kilmainham Gaol Archives.
16. Prisoners Petitions and Correspondence 2304, Irish State Paper Office.
17. Prisoners Petitions and Correspondence 2860, Irish State Paper Office.
18. Prisoners Petitions and Correspondence 3724, Irish State Paper Office.
19. Report, Inspectors General of Prisons, 1827, National Library of Ireland, Dublin.
20. Registered Papers, 1831 A – 191, Irish State Paper Office.
21. Registered Papers, 1828 T – 733, Irish State Paper Office.
22. Report, Inspectors General of Prisons, 1830, National Library of Ireland, Dublin. All of the above are now in Kilmainham Gaol Archives.

Chapter Ten

1. Report, Inspectors General of Prisons, 1830, National Library of Ireland, Dublin.

2. Kilmainham Gaol Register for 1830, Public Records Office, Dublin.

3. See Kilmainham Gaol Registers covering appropriate periods.

4. *The Making of Modern Ireland*, J.C.Beckett, Faber and Faber, London, 1966.

5. Registered Papers, 1833/G 10, 162, Irish State Paper Office.

6. Acts 1 and 2 George IV. Cap 33 amended.

7. Kilmainham Gaol Register, 1834, Public Records Office, Dublin.

8. Report, Inspectors General of Prisons, 1848, National Library of Ireland, Dublin.

9. Act Victoria Regina 1. Cap 6.

10. Act Victoria Regina 8 & 9. Cap 107.

11. Report, Inspectors General of Prisons, 1841, National Library of Ireland, Dublin.

12. Act Victoria Regina 5 & 6. Cap 95.

13. Facsimile documents relating to the famine available at the Public Records Office, Dublin.

14. Act Victoria Regina for the Prevention of Crime and Outrage in Ireland, No. 11, Cap. 2.

15. Peter Carolan, my colleague at Kilmainham was very excited at the find, and the Bible is now in the Kilmainham Gaol Archives.

16. Kilmainham Gaol Register for year 1848, Public Records Office, Dublin.

Chapter Eleven

1. *Dublin*, Peter Somerville Large, Hamish Hamilton, London, 1970.

2. Kilmainham Gaol Register for year 1849, Public Records Office, Dublin.

3. Report, Inspectors General of Prisons, 1848, National Library of Ireland, Dublin.

4. Kilmainham Gaol Register covering the periods 1848,1849, 1850, 1851, Public Records Office, Dublin.

5. Report, Inspectors General of Prisons, 1857, National Library of Ireland, Dublin.

6. Note by Thomas Miley, second class turnkey, found at the back of the Gaol Register, 1850, Public Records Office, Dublin.

7. *The Fabrication of Virtue*, Robin Evans, Cambridge University Press, 1982.

8. Plan of Pentonville Prison, as reproduced in *The Fabrication of Virtue*, Robin Evans, Cambridge University Press, 1982.

9. Plan of Kilmainham Gaol, circa 1857, found in the gaol and now forming part of the Kilmainham Gaol Archives.

10. Biographical notes on the Architect, John McCurdy, from the Architectural Archives, Dublin.

11. Act Victoria Regina. Cap. XCIX, 20 August 1823, amended 1857.

12. Act Victoria Regina. Cap. LXV 111, Section 7.

13. Report, Inspectors General of Prisons, 1862, National Library of Ireland, Dublin.

14. Sometimes called the Judas Hole and a feature of every cell door in all prisons of the period.

15. *The Fabrication of Virtue*, Robin Evans, Cambridge University Press, 1982.

16. Stonebreaking was the most profitable area of many gaols – the stones being sold to contractors for the reconstruction of roads and walls. During the reconstruction of the road from Kilmainham to Inchicore during the late 1850s the stones were supplied under contract from Kilmainham Gaol by arrangement between the Governor and Contractor.

Chapter Twelve

1. A secret association established in America in 1858 called 'The Fenians', out of which came the Irish Republican Brotherhood, founded in Dublin on 18 March 1858 by Thomas Clarke Luby and James Stephens. The oath of membership ran: 'In the presence of Almighty God I solemnly swear allegiance to the Irish Republic and to take up arms when called on to defend its independence and integrity.'

2. Founded in Dublin, November 1863 under the direction of James Stephens, John O'Leary and Charles Kickham.

3. Report on escape of James Stephens, carried out by Inspectors General of Prisons, from their office now situated at Dublin Castle, dated 7 December, 1865, signed James Lentaigne and Larry Connellan, with plan of Richmond Prison attached in appendix form.

4. The total cost of new locks, check gates, bolts, hasps, etc., was £802-16-5, Report, Inspectors General of Prisons, 1865, National Library of Ireland.

5. The Kilmainham Papers, now in the National Library of Ireland.

6. Kilmainham Gaol Register, 1866. Public Records Office, Dublin.

7. Kilmainham Gaol Register, 1866. Public Records Office, Dublin.

8. Documents relating to Fenianism, Irish State Paper Office.

9. Kilmainham Gaol Register, from March to April 1867 had an average arrest and charge rate of sixty prisoners a day, while few were released after questioning.

10. Habeas Corpus Suspension Act, abstracts of cases, Irish State Paper Office – all in alphabetical order.

11. Description of Governor Price's design, as contained in Report, Inspectors General of Prisons, to Lord Lieutenant, dated July 1868, in Official Papers, 1868, Irish State Paper Office.

12. Report, Inspectors General of Prisons, 1872, National Library of Ireland, Dublin.

13. Kilmainham Gaol Register, 1872, Public Records Office, Dublin, and Inspectors General Reports on discipline in annual report, same year,

National Library of Ireland.

Chapter Thirteen

1.   Document of Establishment and Inauguration of General Prisons Board
      lent by courtesy of Governor's Office, Mountjoy Prison.

2.   Standing Orders, General Prison Board of Ireland, now returned to
      Mountjoy Prison.

3.   Five Year Report, General Prison Board of Ireland, 1878-1883, Irish
      State Paper Office.

4.   Standing Orders, General Prison Board of Ireland, in relation to the
      division of the day, for categories of prisoners, not political, lent by
      Mountjoy Prison.

5.   *Kilmainham Memories*, Tadhg Hopkins, Ward Lock, 1896.

6.   Five year report, General Prison Board of Ireland 1878-1883, Irish State
      Paper Office.

7.   From Belfast, transferred during his sentence to Mountjoy Convict Depot,
      November 1882. Register of Mountjoy Prison, Public Records Office,
      Dublin.

8.   The inscription places the erection of the altar in 1882 when it must
      have replaced an earlier one. Some time after the closing of the prison
      in 1924, the altar was removed to Arbour hill. It was returned to
      Kilmainham and re-erected in 1970. The wooden altar rails, made in
      the eighteenth century were originally in the Carmelite Church,
      Clarendon Street and were presented to Kilmainham by the Carmelite
      Order in 1973.

9.   Standing Orders, General Prison Board, now returned to Mountjoy Prison.

10.   *A Dictionary of Irish Biography*, Henry Boylan, Gill and MacMillan,
      1978.

11.   See letter from Charles Stewart Parnell dated 23 October 1881, to the
      Editor of the *Freeman's Journal* newspaper, written from Kilmainham
      Gaol in which he states the unanimous feeling of every man in the gaol
      as willing to remain there as long as necessary and as long as the Irish
      people stood by the lessons learned by the Land League.

12.   See map of Kilmainham Gaol, circa 1857 reproduced in this book on page
      85. All political prisoners had their cells cleaned for them by prisoners
      assigned to 'domestic duties'. It was considered a prestigious position to
      undertake this task.

13.   By the passing of this bill it became law that if rent due in 1881 was
      paid and if there were arrears previous to this date which the tenant
      farmer was clearly unable to pay, arrears would be cancelled by the
      payment of half the amount due, with the entire amount not being in
      excess of one year's rent. *A Consideration of Ireland in the 18th Century*,
      page 397 – Locker Lampson, Constable, London, 1907.

14. Forster appointed 10 May 1880, resigned 3 May 1882. Cavendish was married to a niece of premier Gladstone.

15. The five men are buried in the yard of the prison known as the Invincibles Yard. On examination no marks indicate the spot either on the flagstones or on the prison wall itself.

16. Standing Orders, General Prison Board of Ireland, in relation to procedures to be followed for the preparation of an execution, now returned to Mountjoy.

Chapter Fourteen

1. Five year report, ending 1910 General Prisons Board, Irish State Paper Office.

2. Edward Carson, also prosecuting Counsel in the trial of Oscar Wilde. Both were students together in Trinity College, Dublin.

3. William Martin Murphy, Proprietor, *Irish Independent*, and Director of the Dublin Tramway Company.

4. Joseph Mary Plunkett and Roger Casement sent to Germany to enlist aid.

5. Father Augustine was not allowed to accompany Pearse to the place of execution, instead parted with him at the entrance to the yard.

6. This letter indicates that Pádraig had no idea his young brother was to share his fate.

7. Father McCarthy had his presbytery in James Street. He was Roman Catholic Chaplain to Kilmainham.

8. Michael O'Hanrahan was a member of the Second Battalion, which had occupied Jacobs Factory. His brother Jack fought beside him and was taken prisoner to Kilmainham. He received a sentence of death, later commuted to penal servitude.

9. Both were parents of Seán MacBride, our Nobel Peace Prize winner. He was 12 at the time of his father's execution, and was told the news by his headmaster. Young Seán MacBride was at school in Paris, conversation with Seán MacBride, June 1987.

10. Later Mrs R. Muleahy, Dublin.

11. From *Last Words* by Piaras MacLochlainn, Kilmainham Gaol Restoration Society.

12. Originally the boundary wall (see illustration page 27) before enlargements completed 1864.

13. For a detailed account of the escape, and Kilmainham experiences, see *On Another Man's Wound* by Ernie O'Malley, Anvil Books, 1936.

14. From author's conversations with Sheila Humphries, a prisoner in Kilmainham during 1923, arrested because of family friendship with Ernie O'Malley. The mural in the cell in the Museum Compound bearing Grace Plunkett's name is her own work.

15. The spot is marked by a cross between the wall of the stonebreaker's yard and the stern of the *Asgard*.

Acknowledgements

I confess that I entered into the writing of this book almost by accident. I was at the time furthering my interest in the rebellion and personality attached to Robert Emmet and 1803 but consistently found myself during those times within the awesome confines of Kilmainham Gaol.

In spite of my feelings of incompetence at the undertaking of such a mammoth task, I was encouraged by very many people whose generosity and kindness provided me with the incentive to carry on.

For assistance with my research I am deeply indebted to the staffs of the Public Records Office, Dublin and the Irish State Paper Office, Dublin Castle, the Gilbert Memorial Library, Pearse Street and the National Library of Ireland, Kildare Street, all of whom showed me particular courtesy and consideration over a period of two years of research. My thanks to Paul Hogan of the National Museum who provided me with information on the period 1916-1923.

An enormous debt of gratitude is due to my colleagues at Kilmainham Gaol, in particular to Amanda Crawford for her expert knowledge of Theobald Wolfe Tone and the Society of the United Irishmen; to my friend and colleague John Nolan for his invaluable assistance at all stages of the task on hand, but in particular for his help and guidance in relation to the rebellion of 1803.

Thanks to Martin Crawford for his painstaking efforts at bringing back to life in visual form so many aspects of Kilmainham which in effect had disappeared. His commitment and enthusiasm to the project was a much sustaining factor to me personally.

Thanks to Patrick Long and Peter Carolan for confirmation of facts in relation to the Young Irelanders' Rising and

Kilmainham 1848, and again to John Nolan for his valuable contribution of the Fenian period.

My appreciation to Patricia Valentine for the benefit of her knowledge of the Parnell and Invincibles period in Kilmainham, to Dan and Helen Magill, nor could I fail to omit my friend Mark Hyland, who introduced me to Kilmainham as a guide, eights years ago.

Thanks to my friends Hugh Bradley, Ann Nolan, Jacqueline and Brendan Halpin, Damien, Clare and Trudy McHugh, Rita Whyte, Dolores Bindokas, Gabrielle and Andy Sweeney, Kay and Larry Judge and to the Royal Hospital Kilmainham, in particular to Vivien Igoe, who provided me with much assistance and determination of purpose by friendship and encouragement.

A very special word of thanks to John Lonergan, Governor, Mountjoy Prison, for his foreword, and for opening prison doors; to chief Prison Officer, James Petherbridge, Mountjoy and to Officer Derek Brennan, who combined to provide me with an insight into the machinations of the present prison system.

I am deeply indebted to Frank Sherlock, Instructor at the Training Unit, Glengarriff Parade and to Liam C. Manus also of the Training Unit, whose knowledge of prison architecture equipped me with a clear perspective of the design and structure of prisons of the time. I want to acknowledge especially the assistance of Derek Green, Architect, Office of Public Works, Stephen's Green who guided me through the changing facade of Kilmainham, map by map and who never once lost his patience with my questioning or with my demands on his time.

This manuscript would never have reached completion without the support of Eithne Mulhern, also of Mountjoy Prison, who dedicated an enormous amount of her free time in faultlessly placing it in typescript and whose helpful suggestions right throughout the course of my work made the task on hand that much easier. For those months of co-operation and for everyone's friendship and goodwill, I shall always be grateful.

A special word of thanks to my brother Seán for giving of his time and for his photography and to his wife, Anne-Helena.

Nobody better than my friends Nell and Nino Caffola know of how many times I very nearly gave up and who opened doors of comfort and inspiration to me when faced with despair. Indeed, to everyone who assisted, I am sincerely grateful.

Finally, I should like to thank the curator of Kilmainham Gaol, Patrick Cooke, who took much trouble with my manuscript in draft form and whose advice and guidance was a constant source of inspiration to me. To John Toolan, Supervisor Guide, Kilmainham, no words of mine could express gratitude for his tireless patience with me at all times during research, and whose belief in what I was doing spurred this work to completion. To Seán Feehan, my publisher and the Mercier Press, I owe a great debt, in particular to Mary Feehan, who edited my manuscript.

Most of all, I should like to thank my daughter Serena for her help and supportive love during the long construction of 'The Dismal House of Little Ease', and without whom, over and above everything and everyone else it would never have reached completion.

Freida Kelly
Kilmainham Gaol
March 1988

More Interesting Titles

The Cultural Conquest of Ireland
Kevin Collins

Most Irish people are aware that a dramatic transformation has occurred in Ireland over the last four centuries. It is significant that the colonists singled out for destruction those aspects of life in which the Irish differed so markedly from the English. It was clear that only the destruction of these cultural traits could pave the way for the absorption of the Irish into the English realm. It is also significant that historians, for the most part, have ignored or dismissed these things, concentrating instead on political events.

The Cultural Conquest of Ireland looks at the spirit behind Irish culture and draws attention to the many neglected aspects of our past – some of which still influence our daily lives.

THE COURSE OF IRISH HISTORY
Edited by T.W. Moody and F.X. Martin

This highly acclaimed book is the first of its kind in its field. It provides a rapid short survey, with a geographical introduction, of the whole course of Ireland's history. Based on a series of Radio Telefís Éireann television programmes it is designed to be both popular and authoritative, concise but comprehensive, highly selective but balanced and fair-minded, critical but constructive and sympathetic. A distinctive feature is its wealth of illustrations.

Milestones in Irish History
Edited by Liam de Paor

This book spans the whole range of time from early pre-history to the present and discusses the great turning points in the history of Ireland, their causes and their consequences. The contributors are Frank Mitchell, Liam de Paor, Donnchadh Ó Corráin, Michael Richter, Margaret MacCurtain, Aidan Clarke, James McGuire, Richard B. Walsh, Kevin B. Nowlan, Joseph Lee, Donal McCartney, Ronan Fanning and John A. Murphy.

MICHAEL COLLINS AND THE TREATY
His differences with de Valera
T. Ryle Dwyer

To Michael Collins the signing of the Treaty between Ireland and Britain in 1921 was a 'stepping stone'. Eamon de Valera called it 'Treason'.

The controversy surrounding this Treaty is probably the most important single factor in the history of this country, not only because it led to the Civil War of 1922–1923 but also because the basic differences between the country's two main political parties stem from the dispute.

T. Ryle Dwyer not only takes an in-depth look at the characters and motivations of the two main Irish protagonists but also gives many insights into the views and ideas of the other people involved on both sides of the Irish Sea.